meat and potatoes

villard | new york

meat and potatoes

52 RECIPES, FROM SIMPLE TO SUBLIME

joan schwartz

A Villard Books Trade Paperback Original

COPYRIGHT © 2003 BY JOAN SCHWARTZ

Library of Congress Cataloging-in-Publication Data

Schwartz, Joan.
    Meat and potatoes: 52 recipes, from simple to sublime /
Joan Schwartz.
        p.   cm.
      ISBN 0-8129-6664-3
      1. Cookery (Meat)   2. Cookery (Potatoes)   I. Title.

TX749.S32   2003
641.6′6—dc21   2003041108

Villard Books website address: www.villard.com

Printed in the United States of America on acid-free paper

9 8 7 6 5 4 3 2 1

Book design by Barbara M. Bachman

In loving memory of my husband,

Allen G. Schwartz

ACKNOWLEDGMENTS

Writing *Meat and Potatoes* has been a pleasure, in large
part because of the talented and generous people who
offered their support and worked along with me from start
to finish. My sincere gratitude to Jane Dystel,
Stacey Glick, Mary Bahr, Laura Ford, Eve Lindenblatt,
Keith Dresser, and David Blasband.

Special thanks to the amazing chefs who contributed their
vision to this book. For me, and for everyone who tastes the
delights that follow, meat and potatoes will never be the same.

Contents

2. BEEF AND POTATOES

3. VEAL, MIXED MEATS, AND POTATOES

4. LAMB, VENISON, AND POTATOES

5. PORK AND POTATOES

meat and potatoes

1.

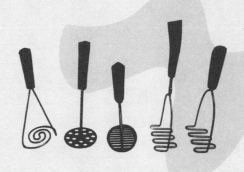

Introducing Meat and Potatoes

*A*DMIT IT, WHEN YOU'RE HUNGRY, YOU WANT MEAT AND potatoes! Put the two together and you need very little else to make a meal; their synergy in a dish always promises sustenance and comfort. But although comfort food was what I was after as I set out to collect recipes from America's finest chefs, I soon learned that the pairing of meat and potatoes goes way beyond the homey and nourishing—it provides a feast for the imagination.

The chefs who contributed to this book work their magic with beef, lamb, veal, and pork, and combine these meats with both white and sweet potatoes (including boniatos, which are a bit of each). The meats are grilled, roasted, braised, fried, or sautéed; the potatoes—whole, sliced, chunked, diced, or mashed—are braised, fried, sautéed, boiled, or simmered. The results are such creative leaps as Slow-Braised Veal and Vanilla Sweet Potato Shepherd's Pie (Gerry Hayden); Beef Short Rib Hash with Sunny Eggs and Balsamic Syrup (Deborah Stanton); Potato-Crusted Lamb Cakes (Daniel Angerer); Indian-Spiced Rack of Lamb with Potato Tikki and Mint Yogurt (Thomas John); and Roasted New Potatoes with Bacon, Chive Flowers, and Green Tomato Dressing (Ilene Rosen).

Much of the time, at home and in restaurants, meat and potatoes are cooked separately and presented together at the table. Grilled steak, for example, is just plain wonderful served with a creamy, herbal potato salad or beside a rich gratin that accents its simple perfection.

But when meat and potatoes are married in the pot, the finished dish is even more complex and nuanced, as with rib-eye steak that is oven-roasted over a bed of potatoes so that the savory and herbal flavors of the meat and its seasonings permeate the potatoes (Mitchel London); mashed potatoes that are formed into crusty cakes and stuffed with chili-spiced, braised short ribs (Andrew DiCataldo); diced potatoes combined with chorizo and layered over tortillas, to make crisp quesadillas (Sue Torres); and jalapeño-spiked mashed sweet potatoes that stuff a tender pork roulade (Glenn Harris).

Cook them separately or cook them together—both approaches show how meat and potatoes can work with one another, each highlighting the qualities of its partner. The final harmonious dish can be hot or cold, spicy or mild, sentimental or cutting edge. Just as macaroni and cheese is always greater than the sum of its parts, so is meat and potatoes.

A few words of advice: Although some of the dishes can be cooked relatively quickly, most of these recipes are not instant. Braises and roasts will require prep time and cooking time, and you should read each recipe carefully and plan ahead. But the good news is that nothing smells as wonderful as meat and potatoes that are gently simmering or roasting along with aromatic vegetables and herbs, wafting an atmosphere of well-being and plenty through your kitchen. Such cooking embodies the best qualities of slow food, whose preparation is a calming and gratifying activity—more pleasure than work and offering rewards you can taste.

Nevertheless, to make them more manageable, many recipes can be broken down into components that are made and refrigerated ahead and combined just before serving. A number of dishes can be cooked ahead and reheated later, and their flavor will deepen and mellow. And the bonus is that when you cook and later reheat, you get to enjoy the sensual experience (but not the work) twice.

As you become acquainted with these recipes, they will feed your own creative talents. Once you feel comfortable with the mechanics of braising, slow-roasting, and grilling, it becomes easy to choose a cut of meat and a variety of potatoes and pair them with the appropriate method. You can invent a recipe from scratch or deconstruct one of ours and reshuffle components to come up with a spontaneously delightful meal. Meat and potatoes are not only inspiring, they are forgiving.

About Meat

Buy the freshest and best-quality meat, from a butcher or supermarket you trust. If possible, buy ground meat from a butcher who grinds it to your order, rather than from a market where it has been preground and wrapped. Of course, check the date carefully on all packaged meat. As soon as possible after purchase, rewrap and refrigerate meat; use ground meat within two days and solid pieces within four days.

You will find that the more tender the cut of meat, the less time it needs to cook. Steaks and chops take only minutes from grill to table, while beef short ribs and oxtails—where flavorful morsels are hidden among the bones and fat—require longer braising. Leg and shoulder of lamb need a good amount of time in the oven to reach optimum flavor and texture. Although you can let each individual recipe be your guide, here are brief descriptions of the cooking methods used in this book:

Braising: Brown the meat in a little oil, then cook, partially submerged in a flavorful liquid, in a heavy, tightly covered pot or pan. Meat can be braised on the stovetop, in a Crock-Pot, or in the oven. Braising is the preferred method for tougher cuts of meat.

Grilling: Light an outdoor charcoal or gas grill and cook the meat quickly at a high temperature. Indoors, you can substitute an electric grill (make sure it provides enough heat to sear the meat), a stovetop grill pan, or a broiler.

Roasting: Cook the meat in a preheated oven, at a moderate to high temperature.

Sautéeing: Cook the meat in a skillet or sauté pan, in oil that has been heated until it shimmers, over medium or medium-high heat. Stir the meat as it cooks.

Stewing: Cover the meat with a flavorful liquid and cook at a simmer. This may be done on the stovetop, in a Crock-Pot, or in the oven.

The following meats are called for in our recipes:

BEEF

Cheeks
Meat near the face of the steer. Cheeks are a rich cut, with a gelatinous texture and a very intense flavor.

Chuck
Juicy and inexpensive cut from the shoulder and neck. Ground chuck goes into stew, meat loaf, and hamburger, and becomes the stuffing for chili peppers.

Oxtail
Tail of the steer; very bony meat. Chunky pieces (not from the end of the tail) are the meatiest, and become flavorful and tender when braised. Generally sold in 1- to 3-inch cross sections.

Rump
A cut from the bottom round; flavorful, a bit tougher than chuck, but very tender when braised.

Short Ribs
Cut from the prime rib and the next lower three ribs, these tasty, meaty ends of beef ribs require long cooking to become tender. They have layers of fat, meat, and bone. Fat must be removed both before and after cooking.

Shoulder

Same as chuck.

Steaks

Filet Mignon: Cut from the beef tenderloin. This is the tenderest steak, but it has a milder flavor than other steaks.

Rib Eye: Cut from the rib section. Juicy, flavorful, marbled with fat; not as tender as filet mignon.

Shell, or Strip Loin, Steak: A boneless cut from the beef short loin. Tender and mild-flavored.

Skirt Steak: Long, narrow steak, cut from the breast. A little fatty, but tender.

LAMB

Chops

Loin: From the hind saddle of the lamb. These are the tenderest lamb chops.

Rib: Cut from the rack. Tender and flavorful.

Shoulder: Cut from the lamb chuck. Juicy and marbled with fat, but not as tender as rib or loin chops. Arm chops, with a round bone, come from the lower part of the shoulder. Blade chops, with a narrow bone, are cut from the beginning of the shoulder.

Leg

Last half of the hind saddle of the lamb. A whole leg weighs from 6 to 11 pounds, but you can buy the shank end, which has more meat and less fat, or the sirloin end, which is tender but has more bone. A leg of lamb can be boned and then either butterflied or rolled and tied.

Rack

The attached lamb ribs, usually seven or eight ribs (each would be a chop if they were separated). The rack, which is the beginning of the foresaddle, is tender and delicious.

Shank

Includes part of the arm chop and bone. The foreshank is meatier than the hind shank.

Shoulder; Boneless Shoulder

A bit less tender than the leg, and more economical. A boneless shoulder can be rolled and roasted.

PORK

Bacon

Very fatty meat from the underside of a pig, sold sliced or in slabs. It is cured and smoked. Applewood-smoked bacon has excellent flavor and texture.

Chorizo

Cuban-style pork sausage made with paprika, wine, sugar, garlic, and fat.

Ham

Cured pork leg or shoulder. Black Forest ham is cut in one piece from the tenderest portion of the ham and smoked over corncobs or pinewood. It has excellent flavor and texture.

Kielbasa

Polish smoked sausage made from pork or a combination of beef and pork (it may also be made from beef).

Loin

The pork loin is divided into the blade end, which has the most fat; the sirloin end, which has the most bone; and the center, tenderloin portion, which is the leanest and most tender.

Tenderloin: The fillet cut from the center of the loin, usually 8 to 12 ounces; lean and tender.

Pancetta

Flavorful, moist Italian bacon that is cured, not smoked. It is usually sold in a sausage shape.

Prosciutto

Italian cured, air-dried ham that is firm, with a delicate flavor.

Breast; Boneless Breast

The breast includes the lower end of the ribs and weighs 9 to 10 pounds with bones. Chewy and flavorful.

Chops

Loin: These are the tenderest veal chops. Tournedos are boneless loin chops, very lean and tender. They are thin, so be careful not to overcook.

Rib: Cut from the rack. Very tender.

Rack, or Veal Rib Roast

The first part of the veal foresaddle, the rack looks like several attached rib chops. The first six bones have the tenderest meat.

About Potatoes

Textural wizards, potatoes can morph from dense to fluffy, chewy to crisp, depending on their preparation. A number of varieties are available at greenmarkets and supermarkets, and for more unusual types, contact the specialty suppliers listed in Sources. In our recipes, each chef states his or her preference, but if it isn't available, feel free to try another potato that is similar.

White (and gold) potatoes are classified as

STARCHY, with high starch and low water content

WAXY, with low starch and high water content

ALL PURPOSE, with medium starch and water content

NEW, with low starch and high water content (harvested when
   young and thin-skinned, these potatoes
   can be of any variety).

More starch generally makes potatoes good for baking, frying, and mashing; less means they are best roasted, boiled, or braised. That said, you may enjoy russet potatoes in some braises, as I do. They crumble a bit as they cook and thicken the sauce.

If you aren't sure which category your spuds fall into, put them in a bowl of salted water (2 tablespoons of salt to 11 ounces of water). High-starch potatoes will sink; waxy potatoes will float.

Shop for tubers that have firm, unwrinkled skin, without sprouts, cuts, or blemishes. Avoid those with green spots under the skin, which indicate that the potatoes have been stored in the light. (In a pinch, green spots, sprouts, and blemishes can be cut off, and the rest of the potato can be cooked.) Remove potatoes from their plastic bag and store them in a pantry that is cool, dark, and well ventilated. Although you should never refrigerate mature white or sweet potatoes, because their starch will convert to sugar, you can refrigerate new potatoes, which are lower in starch.

A general rule is three medium potatoes per pound; each pound makes about 2 cups mashed.

The following potatoes are called for in our recipes:

Peruvian Blue or Purple
Skin and flesh range from blue or lavender to dark purple. They have a dense texture, a subtle flavor, and a medium starch content. They originated in South America.

Boniato, or Cuban Sweet Potato
White-fleshed sweet potatoes that are less sweet than regular sweet potatoes, with a more subtle flavor, and a fluffy texture when cooked. Their skin color ranges from red to tan.

Fingerling
Shaped like a finger, 1 to 8 inches long. These are baby long white potatoes, with thin, light skin and a firm, creamy texture. They are all-purpose, with medium starch.

German Butterball
Yellow-fleshed round or oblong potatoes with a buttery taste, smooth deep yellow skin, and medium starch. This variety originated in Europe and was renamed in the United States.

New

Small, round, red- or brown-skinned potatoes that have been harvested before reaching maturity. They have low starch.

Red Bliss

Small, round, red-skinned new potatoes grown in California, Minnesota, and the Dakotas. They have a firm, smooth texture, white flesh, and less moisture than other red varieties, and they are low in starch. The spring and summer crops are sold immediately and have a sweeter, milder flavor than the fall crop, which is stored for later shipment.

Round Red

"Boiling potatoes." These have reddish-brown skin, waxy flesh, and medium starch.

Ruby Crescent Fingerling

Slightly larger fingerlings with pink-tan skin, yellow flesh, and low starch.

Russet, or Idaho

Rough brown skin with many eyes; white flesh; a light, fluffy texture when cooked; and high starch. This is the most widely used potato variety in the United States.

Sweet

Although there are many varieties, with orange, red, or white flesh, the darker-skinned orange-fleshed potatoes and the paler-skinned yellow-fleshed potatoes are the most common. The orange-fleshed, commonly called yams, are sweet and moist; the yellow-fleshed are less sweet and drier in texture. Both are long and tapered. (True yams are another tuber entirely, not related to sweet potatoes. They are large, starchy, and bland, with white, pink, or yellow flesh.)

Yukon Gold

Tan skin; oval shape; buttery, light yellow flesh; and a creamy texture. These are all-purpose potatoes, with medium starch.

Sources

Most of the ingredients called for in the recipes are available at good supermarkets, specialty stores, butcher shops, ethnic markets, greenmarkets, and farmers' markets. Here are some telephone and Web sources, as well.

Aleppo Pepper

ADRIANA'S CARAVAN: 800-316-0820;
WWW.ADRIANASCARAVAN.COM
DEAN & DELUCA: 800-221-7714; WWW.DEANDELUCA.COM

Beef Cheeks

OTTOMANELLI & SONS: PHONE: 212-675-4217; FAX: 212-620-7286

Borlotti (Cranberry) Beans, Dried

BUONITALIA: 212-633-9090

Chilies, Dried

THE CMC COMPANY: 800-262-2780; WWW.THECMCCOMPANY.COM
CULINARY PRODUCE: 908-789-4700; WWW.CULINARYPRODUCE.COM
KALUSTYANS: 212-685-3451; WWW.KALUSTYANS.COM
PENZEYS: 800-741-7787; WWW.PENZEYS.COM

Chili Powders and Ground Chili Peppers

INTERNATIONAL SPICEHOUSE: 516-942-7248; WWW.SPICEHOUSEINT.COM
KALUSTYANS: 212-685-3451; WWW.KALUSTYANS.COM
PENZEYS: 800-741-7787; WWW.PENZEYS.COM

Demi-Glace

WWW.GATEWAYGOURMET.COM
MORE THAN GOURMET: 800-860-9385; WWW.MORETHANGOURMET.COM

Duck Fat

WWW.LUVADUCK.COM

Galangal

PENZEYS: 800-741-7787; WWW.PENZEYS.COM

Hickory Smoke Powder

INTERNATIONAL SPICEHOUSE: 516-942-7248; WWW.SPICEHOUSEINT.COM

LET'S SPICE IT UP!: 847-433-6309; WWW.LETSSPICEITUP.COM

Kaffir Lime Leaves

IMPORTFOOD.COM: 888-618-THAI; WWW.IMPORTFOOD.COM

Lemongrass

PENZEYS: 800-741-7787; WWW.PENZEYS.COM

Oregano

ADRIANA'S CARAVAN: 800-316-0820; WWW.ADRIANASCARAVAN.COM

Pomegranate Molasses

ADRIANA'S CARAVAN: 800-316-0820; WWW.ADRIANASCARAVAN.COM

KALUSTYANS: 212-685-3451; WWW.KALUSTYANS.COM

Potatoes

CULINARY PRODUCE: 908-789-4700; WWW.CULINARYPRODUCE.COM

(RUBY CRESCENT FINGERLINGS)

WWW.BIGELOWFARMS.COM (GERMAN BUTTERBALLS)

Truffle Butter

WWW.URBANI.COM

Truffle Oil, Black and White

    WWW.URBANI.COM

Truffles, Black

    WWW.URBANI.COM

Venison

    WWW.ATLANTICGAMEMEATS.COM
    WWW.AVENISON.COM
    D'ARTAGNAN: 800-327-8246; WWW.DARTAGNAN.COM

2.

Beef and Potatoes

*R*OBUST AND SATISFYING, BEEF SEEMS TO BE the favorite selection of meat-and-potato chefs. In fact, in sheer number of recipes, beef wins by a landslide, paired imaginatively with Yukon Gold, russet, boniato, red-skinned, purple, fingerling, Red Bliss, sweet, and new potatoes.

Steak is our starting point, the simplest and most tender cut chosen. It needs no more than to be simply grilled or roasted—but every cook has a unique perspective on what makes its best accompaniment. Keep your eye on the potatoes, because they are far more than an embellishment; they provide the variety and flair that define each dish.

Nora Pouillon marinates and grills strip steaks, and complements them with a rich gratin of potatoes, cream, and truffles; Philip McGrath's steak of choice is tender filet mignon, which he combines with the best of summer: beefsteak tomatoes and potato salad tossed with fresh tarragon; and Anita Lo pairs grilled shell steaks with crisp pancakes of grated potatoes stuffed with melted raclette cheese. Mitchel London roasts rib-eye steaks over and surrounded by potatoes, so that some spuds emerge crusty, while others become creamy and infused with meat juices. In a mélange of contrasts, Craig Cupani's steak becomes the center of a salad with portobello mushrooms, sweet caramelized onions, and rösti potatoes stuffed with bacon.

Less tender cuts require longer cooking times than steaks, but they can be made ahead and reheated, and they gain in flavor when served the next day. Short ribs are a favorite for braising: Felino

Samson combines them with creamy mashed boniatos; Laura Frankel incorporates them into the complex flavors of her Moroccan-Spiced Cassoulet; Dan Barber and Michael Anthony braise the ribs and serve them with delicate Ruby Crescent fingerlings. Deborah Stanton braises and minces these meaty ribs and turns them into a surprising Beef Short Rib Hash with Sunny Eggs and Balsamic Syrup; and Andrew DiCataldo treats them to a barbecue spice rub before cooking, in his Spicy Short Rib–Stuffed Potatoes.

Shepherd's pie, traditionally a casserole of savory ground or minced meat topped with buttery mashed potatoes, defines the meat-and-potato genre, but you won't recognize your old favorite in this section (see "Lamb, Venison, and Potatoes" for the classic pie). Here it is reborn three times: with tender braised short ribs and borlotti beans, in Hugh Acheson's dish; with gelatin-rich oxtail, in John Sundstrom's take on the original; and with beef shanks braised in fruity Zinfandel, in Henry Archer Meer's delicious version.

Cyril Renaud introduces us to meltingly tender beef cheeks, served with a super-rich purée of fingerling potatoes. Beef shanks offer rich, meaty flavor, and Arthur Schwartz first roasts them with root vegetables and then braises the oven-browned shanks and vegetables along with potatoes.

Juicy beef chuck, the definitive stew meat, is gently boiled with potatoes and other vegetables Provençal style, by Antoine Bouterin, a master of that cuisine. And Levana Kirschenbaum tells us how to adapt the classic boeuf bourguignon to cooking in a laborsaving Crock-Pot. In the hands of gifted chef Patricia Yeo, chuck becomes exotic Malaysian Beef Rendang with Sweet Potato–Coconut Purée.

Simple ground chuck shows its versatility, as well, moving from Ron Crismon's all-American Crispy Meat Loaf with Chanterelle-Buttermilk Gravy and Potato Gratin, and Matthew Kenney's savory Meat Loaf Stuffed with Mashed Potatoes and Cheddar, to a Tex-Mex favorite from Diana Barrios Treviño, Chiles Rellenos with Warm Mild Tomato Sauce. And if you crave Mediterranean flavors, Keith Dresser introduces us to meat and potatoes Italian style, in his fluffy Potato Gnocchi with Ragù Bolognese.

BEEF

Grilled Rosemary-Marinated New York Strip Steak with Potato Gratin

Makes 4 servings

Nora Pouillon, of Nora, America's first certified organic restaurant, and Asia Nora, in Washington, D.C., infuses steaks with flavor by way of a bold marinade, and pairs them with a creamy, truffle-perfumed potato gratin. She suggests serving this rich combination with the simplest steamed vegetables, such as broccoli or green beans. Try to use organic ingredients.

FOR THE GRILLED ROSEMARY-MARINATED STEAKS:

2 tablespoons tamari or soy sauce
1 tablespoon minced onion
2 tablespoons minced garlic
2 tablespoons olive oil
1 teaspoon minced fresh rosemary

1 (3-inch) piece of fresh ginger, peeled
 and minced
1 tablespoon Dijon mustard
4 New York strip steaks (about
 8 ounces each)

1. In a medium nonreactive bowl, whisk together the tamari, onion, garlic, olive oil, rosemary, ginger, and mustard. Put the steaks in a glass or other nonreactive dish and pour the marinade over them. Allow them to marinate in the refrigerator for at least 2 hours or up to 8 hours.

2. When ready to cook the steaks, bring them to room temperature and preheat the grill or broiler.

3. Grill the steaks to the desired doneness (about 4 minutes on each side for medium-rare).

2 tablespoons unsalted butter, plus extra for
    the gratin dish
1 clove garlic, minced
2 pounds russet potatoes, peeled and sliced
    into 1/2-inch-thick rounds
1/2 teaspoon sea salt

1/4 teaspoon freshly ground black pepper
1/8 teaspoon freshly grated nutmeg
1 to 2 black truffles, thinly sliced or chopped
    (optional; see Sources)
1 cup heavy cream or half-and-half

1. Preheat the oven to 350°F.

2. Butter a shallow, preferably earthenware, dish and sprinkle with the garlic.

3. Layer the potato slices in the dish, sprinkling each layer with the salt, pepper, nutmeg, and black truffles, if using. Pour the cream over the potatoes; it should come three-quarters of the way up the contents of the dish. Dot with the 2 tablespoons butter, cut into small pieces, and bake for 1 to 1 1/2 hours, until the potatoes are soft and the top is browned and crisp.

TO SERVE, place a steak on each plate and accompany with a portion of the gratin.

BEEF

Grilled Filet Mignon with Tarragon Potato Salad, Beefsteak Tomatoes, and Mustard Vinaigrette

Makes 4 servings

Chef McGrath, of the Iron Horse Grill, in Pleasantville, New York, was inspired to create this dish by the backyard barbecues of his youth. He combines the fondly remembered tastes on a single plate—where they most easily and successfully complement one another and present a beautiful picture. His superb potato salad is more than likely to erase your memories of all others.

FOR THE MUSTARD VINAIGRETTE:

5 tablespoons sherry vinegar
3 tablespoons Dijon mustard
1 cup extra-virgin olive oil

Kosher salt
Freshly ground black pepper

Combine the vinegar and the mustard in a small bowl. Slowly whisk in the olive oil. Season to taste with salt and pepper. This makes about 1 1/2 cups; it can be refrigerated for up to 3 days.

FOR THE TARRAGON POTATO SALAD:

2 pounds Yukon Gold potatoes, unpeeled
Kosher salt
4 scallions (white and 3 inches of green),
    minced

1 tablespoon minced fresh tarragon
Freshly ground black pepper
Mustard Vinaigrette

1. Put the potatoes in a saucepan, cover them with cold water, and bring to a boil over medium-high heat. Add salt and cook the potatoes until tender. Drain the potatoes, and when cool enough to handle, peel and cut into large dice.

2. In a large bowl, combine the diced potatoes, scallions, tarragon, and salt and pepper to taste. Toss with enough of the Mustard Vinaigrette to lightly coat the potatoes. Reserve the remaining vinaigrette. If you are going to serve the potato salad soon, cover and leave it at room temperature. Or refrigerate it for up to 1 day.

FOR THE GRILLED FILET MIGNON AND THE TOMATOES:

4 filet mignon steaks (about 8 ounces each)
Kosher salt
Freshly cracked black pepper (see Note)

Freshly cracked mustard seeds (see Note)
4 scallions, ends trimmed
4 beefsteak tomatoes, thickly sliced

1. Preheat the grill or broiler.
2. Season the steaks with salt, pepper, and mustard seeds.
3. Grill the steaks to the desired doneness (6 to 8 minutes on each side for medium-rare), grilling the scallions along with the steaks for 4 to 6 minutes (take care that they do not burn).
4. Arrange the tomatoes in a circle around the rim of each serving plate, season with salt and pepper, and drizzle with about 1 teaspoon of the reserved vinaigrette.

TO SERVE, place a generous scoop of potato salad in the center of each plate and top with a filet mignon. Garnish each steak with a grilled scallion.

NOTE: For cracked black pepper or mustard seeds, wrap peppercorns or seeds in a dish towel and smash them with a heavy pan.

Grilled Shell Steak with Raclette Potato Pancakes

Makes 4 servings

In this extraordinary version of steak and potato pancakes from Chef Lo, of Annisa Restaurant, in Manhattan, the cakes are stuffed with silky wilted leek and creamy melted cheese, and the juicy grilled shell steaks sit atop a rich mustard sauce. The components of this beautiful dish can be done ahead and assembled at the last minute, when the steaks have been grilled.

FOR THE RACLETTE POTATO PANCAKES:

2 large russet potatoes, peeled and
    julienned
Kosher salt
Freshly ground black pepper
Vegetable or canola oil
1 tablespoon unsalted butter

1 large leek (white part only), washed and cut
    into small dice
1 teaspoon combined chopped fresh chives,
    tarragon, thyme, and parsley
4 ounces ripe raw-milk French raclette cheese,
    cut into flat squares

1. Season the julienned potatoes with salt and pepper and put in a strainer set over a bowl. Press down on the potatoes to squeeze out as much liquid as possible.

2. Place four 5-inch, 3-inch-high, ring molds in a large frying pan over high heat. Pour in 1/4 inch of oil, heat, and flip the ring molds so that the oil coats the interior.

3. Divide the potato mixture among the molds and press down with a spatula, gathering up and discarding any strands of potato that go outside the molds. Cook until the bottom of each pancake is golden brown, then flip the filled molds and cook until the cakes are golden brown on the second side. Push the pancakes out of the molds and drain the cakes

on paper towels. Set aside until cool enough to handle. (To make the potato pancakes without molds, form the potato mixture into 4 thick, round, even cakes, and cook as above.)

4. Meanwhile, in a medium frying pan over medium heat, melt the butter and add the diced leek. Season to taste with salt and pepper. Cook until wilted but not browned, and place in a bowl to cool. When the leek has cooled, stir in the chopped chives, tarragon, thyme, and parsley.

5. When the potato pancakes are cool enough to handle, halve each one crosswise. Spread the leek mixture evenly over the 4 bottom halves and top with a square of raclette cheese. Reserve the top halves. You can make the cakes up to this point 3 hours ahead of time, cover loosely, and keep at room temperature.

6. When ready to serve, preheat the oven to 300°F. Place the halved potato pancakes on a baking sheet and put in the oven until the cheese has melted. Reassemble the cakes.

FOR THE SAUCE:

4 tablespoons plus 1 teaspoon unsalted butter
1 shallot, minced
1/2 cup veal stock, or substitute chicken stock
    or canned low-sodium chicken broth

1 tablespoon Dijon mustard
2 tablespoons coarse-grain mustard
Kosher salt
Freshly ground black pepper

In a medium saucepan over medium-high heat, melt 1 teaspoon of the butter and cook the shallot until softened but not colored. Add the stock and cook until reduced by three-quarters. Stir in the Dijon and coarse-grain mustards. Whisk in the remaining butter by tablespoons, making sure each is incorporated before adding the next. Season with salt and pepper and keep warm over very low heat. The sauce can be refrigerated for up to 1 day and reheated before serving.

4 cups loosely packed baby arugula leaves   *1¹/₂ teaspoons extra-virgin olive oil*
¹/₂ teaspoon red wine vinegar

Put the arugula in a large bowl. Combine the vinegar and olive oil and pour over the leaves, tossing to cover the arugula with the mixture.

4 well-marbled shell steaks (about   *Kosher salt*
   8 ounces each)   *Freshly ground black pepper*

Preheat the grill or broiler (alternatively, set a heavy skillet, preferably cast iron, over high heat until it is heated through). Season the steaks with salt and pepper, and grill to the desired doneness (6 to 8 minutes on each side for medium-rare). Allow the steaks to rest in a warm spot, tented with foil, for 5 minutes.

TO SERVE, divide the sauce among 4 plates. Slice each steak ¹/₂ inch thick across the grain and arrange over the sauce. Place a potato pancake on each plate and garnish with the arugula, if desired.

Seared Rib-Eye Steak with Crisp and Creamy Potatoes

Makes 4 servings

You don't always need a grill to make a great steak, as this memorable dish from Mitchel London happily proves. And what is more, oven-roasting steak along with potatoes allows our two favorite foods to cook together in a way that brings out the finest qualities of both.

2 fresh thyme sprigs
Freshly cracked black pepper (see Note)
4 or 5 cloves garlic, unpeeled, crushed with
    the broad end of a knife blade
2 tablespoons extra-virgin olive oil

2 rib-eye steaks, bone in (about
    1 3/4 pounds each)
2 large russet potatoes, unpeeled, thinly sliced
Kosher salt
Chopped flat-leaf parsley

1. In a large bowl, combine the thyme, pepper, garlic, and 1 tablespoon of the olive oil. Add the steaks and cover with the marinade. Marinate for 2 hours at room temperature, or in the refrigerator if the room is very warm.

2. Preheat the oven to 475°F.

3. Place a large, heavy ovenproof pan, preferably cast iron, on the stove over high heat until it becomes very hot. Sear the steaks for 2 minutes on each side and remove from the pan.

4. Reduce the heat to medium, add the remaining 1 tablespoon olive oil to the pan, and heat until very hot. Toss the potatoes with salt and pepper, add to pan, and cook until brown on both sides and nearly cooked through. Place the steaks on top of some of the potatoes, and arrange the remaining potatoes around the steaks. Place the pan in the middle of the preheated oven and cook the steaks to the desired doneness (15 minutes for

medium-rare). The potatoes that have cooked under the steaks will be creamy, and those that surround the steaks will be crisp.

5. Remove the steaks to a cutting board, tent with foil, and let them sit for 5 minutes.

6. Slice the steaks as desired, and serve with the potatoes. Sprinkle with salt and garnish with chopped parsley.

NOTE: For cracked black pepper, wrap peppercorns in a dish towel and smash them with a heavy pan.

Sliced Steak and Mushroom Salad with Caramelized Onions and Bacon-Rösti Potatoes

Makes 6 servings

In this colorful dish, Chef Cupani, of Manhattan's Patroon Restaurant, makes juicy grilled steak the center of a hearty salad with tomatoes, basil, and grilled onions and mushrooms. Alongside (and very much a part of the picture) are crisp potato pancakes filled with bacon and onions.

This recipe is simpler than it may appear at first reading, because several steps can be done ahead. The steak should be marinated for 6 to 12 hours before cooking, and the bacon-and-onion filling for the potato pancake can be prepared 2 to 3 days before using. The potatoes can be baked up to 1 day before you shred them for the pancake.

Start the potato pancake on top of the stove, and just before you put it into the oven to finish cooking, put the steak, onions, and mushrooms on the grill. You can keep the pancake in the warm oven, if necessary, while you complete the salad.

FOR THE MARINATED STEAK:

2 tablespoons finely chopped shallots
1 tablespoon finely chopped garlic
1 tablespoon finely chopped fresh parsley
Freshly ground black pepper

1/2 cup red wine vinegar
1/2 cup packed brown sugar
1 cup olive oil
4 pounds skirt steak

In a large nonreactive bowl, combine the shallots, garlic, parsley, pepper, vinegar, brown sugar, and olive oil. Add the steak, cover, and refrigerate for at least 6 hours or up to 12 hours.

4 large russet potatoes, unpeeled

8 ounces bacon (preferably applewood
    smoked), cut into small dice

2 large white onions, sliced

Kosher salt

Freshly ground black pepper

Black truffle oil (optional; see Sources)

1 tablespoon chopped flat-leaf parsley

2 tablespoons olive oil

1. Preheat the oven to 400°F.

2. Bake the potatoes for 45 to 50 minutes, until cooked through but not quite soft. The baked potatoes can be refrigerated for up to 1 day.

3. Let the potatoes cool (if you haven't refrigerated them); peel and shred coarsely, using a box grater or a food processor.

4. In a large skillet over medium heat, sauté the bacon for 5 minutes. Discard the excess fat, add the onions, and continue cooking until the onions are dark golden brown, about 15 minutes. Season with salt, pepper, and truffle oil, if using, and stir in the chopped parsley. The bacon-and-onion mixture can be refrigerated for up to 3 days.

5. Preheat the oven to 200°F.

6. Place a 12-inch ovenproof skillet, preferably cast iron, over medium-high heat, add the olive oil, and heat until almost smoking. Add half the shredded potatoes, lightly shaking the pan. Spread the bacon-and-onion mixture evenly over the potatoes, and cover with the remaining grated potatoes. Using a rubber spatula, scrape down the sides of the skillet to keep the potato mixture uniform and round. Keep the pan on the stove just long enough to shape the potato pancake, then put the skillet in the oven for 15 minutes.

7. Carefully remove the skillet from the oven, and using a spatula, flip the potato pancake over (the potato should be golden brown). Return the skillet to the oven for an additional 15 minutes. Remove the potato pancake from the skillet. You can keep the pancake in the warm oven until ready to serve.

Kosher salt
3 red onions, sliced 1/4 to 1/2 inch thick
4 portobello mushrooms, caps only
3 plum tomatoes, sliced into 1/4- to
    1/2-inch-thick rounds

10 fresh basil leaves
Freshly ground black pepper
Olive oil

1. Preheat the grill or broiler.

2. Remove the steak from the marinade and shake off the excess liquid. Season the steak with salt, and grill to the desired doneness (3 to 4 minutes on each side for medium-rare). Grill the onions and mushrooms for 3 to 4 minutes on each side.

3. Remove the steak from the grill and let it sit, tented with foil, for 5 minutes; slice crosswise 1/4 inch thick. Slice the mushrooms crosswise 1/2 inch thick.

4. In a large bowl, separate the grilled onions into rings. Add the sliced mushrooms, plum tomatoes, fresh basil leaves, and finally, the sliced steak. Season with salt, pepper, and a little olive oil, and mix well.

TO SERVE, cut the warm potato pancake into wedges and divide among 6 plates. Evenly distribute the sliced steak and mushroom salad among the plates.

BEEF

Bomboa's Braised Short Ribs with Mashed Boniatos and Gingered Baby Bok Choy

Makes 4 servings

If you haven't yet tried mashed boniatos, you are about to discover something wonderful. In Chef Samson's dish from Chicago's Bomboa Restaurant, the boniatos are unbelievable and the ribs are tender and tasty. Crisp bok choy is a simple companion to this Brazilian-accented combination.

While the meat is cooking, you can prepare the boniatos, and when it is just about done, you can quickly cook the bok choy. When shopping for boniatos in your supermarket, ask for white sweet potatoes—the tubers are often easier to find by that name.

FOR THE BRAISED SHORT RIBS:

4 beef short ribs (10 to 12 ounces each)
Kosher salt
Freshly ground black pepper
2 tablespoons canola oil
2 carrots, finely chopped
1 onion, finely chopped

2 to 3 stalks celery, finely chopped
1 (750-milliliter) bottle red wine
1/4 cup packed light brown sugar
6 cups veal stock, or substitute beef stock
or canned low-sodium beef broth

1. Preheat the oven to 325°F.
2. Season the short ribs all over with salt and pepper.
3. In a large casserole or a roasting pan over medium-high heat, heat the canola oil and brown the meat (4 to 5 minutes on each side).

4. Combine the carrots, onion, and celery (this is a *mirepoix*) and add the vegetables to the meat. Reduce the heat to medium and cook until the vegetables are softened but not browned and some moisture has evaporated, about 5 minutes. Add the red wine and simmer for 5 minutes.

5. In a large saucepan, combine the brown sugar, 1 tablespoon of pepper, and the veal stock and bring to a boil. Pour the boiling stock over the meat and vegetables and cook in the oven, tightly covered, for about 2 hours, or until the meat is tender.

6. Strain, reserving the meat and the braising liquid separately. Discard the solids.

FOR THE MASHED BONIATOS:

4 boniatos (about 2 pounds), peeled
  and quartered
3 tablespoons unsalted butter

1/4 cup heavy cream
Kosher salt
Freshly ground black pepper

Put the boniatos in a large saucepan, cover with cold water, and bring to a boil over high heat. Boil gently until tender, 20 to 30 minutes. Drain and mash the boniatos, or put them through a food mill or ricer into a mixing bowl. Mix in the butter and cream, and season with salt and pepper

4 baby bok choy, split lengthwise
2 tablespoons extra-virgin olive oil
1 teaspoon grated or finely chopped
    fresh ginger

Kosher salt
Freshly ground black pepper

1. Bring a large pot of salted water to a boil and blanch the bok choy for 1 minute. Drain.

2. In a large sauté pan over medium heat, heat the olive oil, add the bok choy, and stir. Add the ginger, season with salt and pepper, and stir or toss to combine well; cook for about 2 minutes. The bok choy should be well coated and just lightly cooked.

TO SERVE, place a large mound of mashed boniatos in the center of each plate. Make a well and sink a short rib into the center of each mound of boniatos. Spoon the braising liquid on and around the meat and potatoes, and accompany with the bok choy.

Braised Short Ribs with Pan-Roasted Ruby Crescent Fingerlings

BEEF

Makes 8 servings

In this winning combination from Manhattan's Blue Hill Restaurant, Chefs Barber and Anthony braise short ribs until the meat is meltingly tender, and combine it with golden pan-roasted fingerling potatoes, the best the greenmarket or your nearest farm stand has to offer.

FOR THE BRAISED SHORT RIBS:

10 pounds beef short ribs
Kosher salt
Freshly ground black pepper
2 tablespoons vegetable oil, plus more
    as needed
2 large onions, coarsely chopped
2 carrots, sliced 1 inch thick
2 stalks celery, sliced 1 inch thick
1 head garlic, unpeeled, halved crosswise

1/4 cup packed dark brown sugar
2 tablespoons Worcestershire sauce
2 fresh bay leaves, or substitute dried
2 cups red wine
1 cup Madeira, or substitute another cup
    of red wine
About 8 cups chicken stock or canned
    low-sodium chicken broth, or
    substitute water

1. Preheat the oven to 225°F.

2. Season the short ribs all over with salt and pepper.

3. In a large sauté pan over high heat, heat the vegetable oil and sear the short ribs until golden brown. You will have to do this in batches. Remove the ribs from the pan and set aside.

4. Pour off all but 2 tablespoons of the fat remaining in the pan. Reduce the heat to low and add the onions, carrots, celery, and garlic to the sauté pan. Gently sauté until the onions are golden, about 5 minutes.

5. Put the reserved ribs and the sautéed vegetables in a deep roasting pan or a Dutch oven. Add the brown sugar, Worcestershire sauce, bay leaves, red wine, and Madeira, and season to taste with salt and pepper. Add enough stock to cover the ribs. Tightly cover the pan with foil and/or a lid. Cook in the oven for 3 to 3½ hours, until the meat separates from the bones.

6. Remove the ribs from the pan and pull the meat from the bones; reserve the meat.

7. In the roasting pan over medium high heat, bring the braising liquid to a gentle boil and reduce it until thick and saucelike. Strain the liquid and return the meat and the liquid to the pan until ready to serve.

FOR THE PAN-ROASTED RUBY CRESCENT FINGERLINGS:

16 Ruby Crescent fingerling potatoes, unpeeled
(see Sources; or substitute another
variety of fingerling, or Red Bliss)
Kosher salt

2 tablespoons olive oil
1 clove garlic, crushed with the broad end of a
knife blade and peeled
Freshly ground black pepper

1. Put the potatoes in a large pot and cover with cold water by 1 inch. Add 1 tablespoon of salt and bring to a gentle boil. Cook the potatoes until tender, 40 to 45 minutes. Drain the potatoes, and peel them while they are still warm. Leave the potatoes whole if they are small; halve or quarter them if they are larger.

2. In a large skillet over medium-high heat, heat the oil with the garlic, and sauté the potatoes until golden, about 4 minutes on each side. Season with salt and pepper.

TO SERVE,   divide the meat with its juices among 8 plates and accompany with the potatoes.

Moroccan-Spiced Cassoulet

Makes 6 to 8 servings

This is a glorious potpourri of Middle Eastern and traditional Western flavors, from Laura Frankel's Manhattan restaurant, Shallots, and its Chicago sibling. You can prepare this cassoulet ahead, relax, and then reheat it when you are ready to serve a truly special meal.

Olive oil

10 pounds short ribs, each rib cut into thirds and trimmed of excess fat (the butcher can do this)

Kosher salt

Freshly ground black pepper

2 large Spanish onions, cut into small dice

3 leeks (white and tender green parts), washed and thinly sliced

4 cloves garlic, crushed with the broad end of a knife blade, peeled, and finely chopped

2 sweet potatoes, peeled and cut into small dice

2 Yukon Gold potatoes, peeled and cut into small dice

1 butternut squash, peeled, seeded, and cut into small dice

1 acorn squash, peeled, seeded, and cut into small dice

3 cups beef or chicken stock, or substitute canned low-sodium beef or chicken broth, plus more as needed

1/2 cup pearl barley

1/4 cup tomato paste

1 tablespoon ground cinnamon

1 tablespoon ground coriander

1/2 teaspoon red pepper flakes

1/2 teaspoon ground cumin

1/4 cup chopped pitted Medjool dates

1/4 cup chopped dried apricots

1/4 cup chopped dried figs (preferably Calimyrna)

1/4 cup chopped fresh parsley

1. Coat the bottom of a large Dutch oven or heavy casserole with olive oil and set the pot over medium-high heat.

2. Season the short ribs all over with salt and pepper and brown them in batches in the oil (adding more oil if needed). Remove the browned ribs to a large roasting pan, and pour off the fat from the pot. Wipe out the pot with paper towels.

3. Preheat the oven to 325°F.

4. Coat the bottom of the Dutch oven with fresh olive oil, place over medium heat, and cook the onions, leeks, and garlic, stirring occasionally, until golden, about 10 minutes. Add the onion mixture to the roasting pan, and repeat the cooking with the sweet potatoes, Yukon Gold potatoes, butternut squash, and acorn squash. Cook all the vegetables in small batches, so as not to overcrowd the Dutch oven, adding olive oil as needed, and seasoning each batch with salt and pepper. Add each cooked batch to the roasting pan.

5. Meanwhile, put the stock and barley in a medium pot and simmer over medium-high heat until the barley is cooked through, about 30 minutes.

6. Add the tomato paste to the Dutch oven and cook quickly until it darkens, 2 to 3 minutes. Stir in the cinnamon, coriander, red pepper flakes, and cumin and cook for 1 to 2 minutes. Add the stock and cooked barley. Add the dates, apricots, and figs.

7. Add the tomato mixture to the roasting pan, and mix well with the meat and vegetables. Add more stock, if needed, to come three-quarters of the way up the contents of the pan. Cover the pan tightly, place it in the oven, and cook for 2 hours.

8. Pour the meat and vegetables into a strainer set over a large bowl and return the strained juices to the roasting pan. Return the cooked vegetables to the pan. Pull the meat from the rib bones, removing the excess fat, and add the meat to the vegetables and juices. Cover the roasting pan and return it to the oven to cook for about 30 minutes more.

9. To serve, divide the meat and vegetables among 6 to 8 plates and spoon the juices over them. Sprinkle with the chopped parsley.

Short Rib Shepherd's Pies with Borlotti Beans and Chive Potato Crust

BEEF

Makes 4 servings

Try these individual shepherd's pies from the Five-and-Ten Restaurant, in Athens, Georgia, the creation of Chef Hugh Acheson. In his imaginative take on what has surely become our favorite cut for braising, savory short ribs are mixed with sturdy pink-flecked beans and then covered with a golden crust of creamy mashed potatoes. The defining herbal flavors here are chives, rosemary, and thyme.

FOR THE SHORT RIBS AND BORLOTTI BEANS:

1 cup dried borlotti (cranberry) beans, rinsed
and picked over (see Sources; or
substitute 2 cups drained canned
Roman beans such as Goya brand)
3 pounds beef short ribs, trimmed of excess fat
Kosher salt
Freshly ground black pepper
2 tablespoons vegetable oil
1 onion, diced

1 carrot, diced
1/2 cup diced celery
2 cups red wine
2 cups chicken or beef stock, or substitute
canned low-sodium chicken or
beef broth
1 bay leaf
1 tablespoon chopped fresh thyme
1 tablespoon chopped fresh rosemary

1. Quick-soak the beans, if desired (see Note).
2. Preheat the oven to 325°F.
3. Season the short ribs all over with salt and pepper.
4. In a large ovenproof pot over medium-high heat, heat the vegetable oil until very hot and sear the ribs on all sides. Remove them to a plate.

5. Pour off all but 1 tablespoon of the oil from the pot and add the onion, carrot, and celery. Sauté the vegetables over medium heat for 5 minutes; they will turn lightly golden and release some of their sugars.

6. Add the wine, increase the heat to medium-high, and cook, scraping the browned bits from the bottom of the pan. Add the stock and bring to a gentle boil. Reduce the heat to medium and bring the mixture to a simmer.

7. Return the ribs to the pot, add the bay leaf, thyme, and rosemary, and cover the pot tightly. Braise in the oven for 2¹/₂ hours.

8. While the ribs are cooking, put the beans in a pot, cover with cold water by 2 inches, and bring to a boil. Skim off any foam that rises, reduce the heat to medium, and simmer the beans, covered, until cooked, about 35 minutes if they have been quick-soaked, 45 to 90 minutes if they haven't. When the beans have softened, add 2 teaspoons salt. Drain and set aside.

FOR THE CHIVE POTATO CRUST:

2 pounds Yukon Gold potatoes, peeled
Kosher salt
3 tablespoons unsalted butter, at room
    temperature

1 cup heavy cream
Freshly ground black pepper
¹/₂ cup chopped fresh chives

Put the potatoes in a saucepan, cover them with cold water, and bring to a boil over medium-high heat. Add 1 tablespoon salt and cook the potatoes until tender. Drain and pass the potatoes through a food mill or ricer into a mixing bowl. While they are still hot, add the butter and cream, combine well, and season with salt and pepper. Fold in the chives.

1. Remove the ribs from the pot and strain the braising liquid. Return the pot, with the braising liquid, to the stove and reduce by half over medium heat. Turn off the heat and add the cooked borlotti beans to the reduced braising liquid. Pull the meat from the rib bones, removing the excess fat, and add the meat to the braising liquid.

2. Increase the oven heat to 400°F.

3. Divide the meat, beans, and braising liquid evenly among 4 ovenproof bowls or small casseroles. Top each with a layer of mashed potatoes and smooth the potatoes over with a knife. Place the 4 bowls on a baking sheet and bake in the oven for 15 minutes.

NOTE: To quick-soak the borlotti beans, put the beans in a small pot and pour boiling water over them to cover by 2 inches. Soak until the beans have doubled in size, about 1 hour. Drain and discard the soaking liquid. Set the beans aside until ready to cook.

Spicy Short Rib–Stuffed Potatoes

Makes 10 appetizer or 5 main-dish servings

Short ribs are treated to a spicy and sweet barbecue rub before they are braised in stock and dark beer; then the tender meat becomes the filling for crusty potato cakes that combine crisp, creamy, chewy, sweet, and spicy in each mouthful. Chef DiCataldo, of Patria, in Manhattan, suggests serving these satisfying cakes with a simple green salad sprinkled with some blue cheese.

You can make the ribs in advance and refrigerate or freeze them in their cooking liquid. If you do this, don't reduce the liquid completely, and finish the reduction when you reheat the meat.

FOR THE BARBECUE SPICE RUB:

1/4 cup granulated sugar
1/4 cup packed light brown sugar
1/4 cup kosher salt
2 tablespoons garlic powder
2 tablespoons onion powder
1/4 cup paprika
2 tablespoons ground ancho chili pepper
     (see Sources)

1 tablespoon ground cumin
2 tablespoons ground chipotle pepper
     (see Sources)
2 tablespoons mulatto (dark American)
     chili powder (see Sources)
1 tablespoon hickory smoke powder
     (see Sources)

Combine all the ingredients and store at room temperature in an airtight container. You will have more than you need for this recipe, but the spice rub will keep for up to 6 months. Makes about 1 1/2 cups.

2 pounds beef short ribs, trimmed of excess fat

1/4 cup Barbecue Spice Rub

1/4 cup canola oil

1 (12-ounce) bottle dark beer, such as Guinness

4 cups chicken stock or canned low-sodium
    chicken broth

1 onion, cut into large chunks

3 cloves garlic, peeled

2 stalks celery, cut into large pieces

3 carrots, cut into large pieces

2 bay leaves

3 tablespoons chopped fresh thyme leaves

Kosher salt

Freshly ground black pepper

1. Rub the short ribs generously with the Barbecue Spice Rub and refrigerate, covered (or in a Ziploc bag), for at least 4 hours or up to 12 hours.

2. Preheat the oven to 350°F.

3. Heat the canola oil in a large, heavy, ovenproof pot over medium-high heat and brown the ribs, turning to cook on all sides (because of the spice rub, they will turn deep brown). Add the beer, stock, onion, garlic cloves, celery, carrots, bay leaves, and thyme, and bring to a boil. Season with 1 1/2 teaspoons salt and 1/2 teaspoon pepper. Loosely top with foil and place in the oven until the meat is very tender and falling off the bone, about 2 1/2 hours.

4. Remove the short ribs from the pot with tongs and put them on a plate or into a high-sided pan. Strain the braising liquid and discard the solids. Return the liquid to the pot and simmer over medium-high heat until the liquid is reduced by half, 25 to 30 minutes. Season with salt and pepper. Shred the meat, discarding the bones and excess fat, and add the meat to the reduced braising liquid. Allow the mixture to cool slightly.

FOR THE MASHED POTATOES:

3 pounds purple potatoes or white baking
    potatoes, unpeeled

Kosher salt

Freshly ground black pepper

Place the potatoes in a large pot and cover with cold water by 1 inch. Add 1 tablespoon salt and bring to a gentle boil. Cook the potatoes until tender, 40 to 45 minutes. Drain the potatoes, let them cool slightly, and peel them. Put the potatoes through a food mill or ricer, or mash them, and season to taste with salt and pepper. Divide the mashed potatoes into 10 equal portions.

FOR THE STUFFED POTATO CAKES:

1/2 cup all-purpose flour
4 large eggs, beaten
Kosher salt

3 cups plain bread crumbs
Canola oil

1. Dip your hands into cold water to prevent the potatoes from sticking. Flatten 1 portion of mashed potatoes between the palms of your hands into a circle 3 1/2 to 4 inches in diameter. Make a slight well in the center and fill it with 2 heaping teaspoons of the braised short ribs, reserving the sauce. Fold the potato circle over the meat. Press the edges together to seal, and with both hands, shape the potato cake into a ball and flatten slightly. Repeat until all the stuffed potato cakes have been formed.

2. Set out 3 medium bowls. Put the flour into one, beat the eggs lightly with 2 teaspoons salt in another, and put the bread crumbs into the third. Dredge the cakes in the flour, gently shaking off the excess. Dip them into the beaten eggs, and roll them in the bread crumbs until they are well coated.

3. Pour canola oil about 1/2 inch deep into a large saucepan or a large, high-sided skillet. Over medium-high heat, heat the oil to 375°F. Carefully put the potato cakes into the hot oil and fry them until golden, about 1 minute on each side. You may have to do this in batches.

4. Remove the cakes from the oil with a slotted spoon, and drain on paper towels. Serve with the reserved sauce.

Beef Short Rib Hash with Sunny Eggs and Balsamic Syrup

Makes 6 servings

Chef Deborah Stanton, of Deborah, in Greenwich Village, has been praised for spinning classics into gold, and this recipe demonstrates her wizardry. It takes simple beef hash to new levels—and it will become your favorite brunch or Sunday supper dish. The balsamic syrup, short ribs, and potatoes can be made ahead and refrigerated, making the final preparation simple and quick.

FOR THE BALSAMIC SYRUP:

2 cups balsamic vinegar

In a small saucepan over very low heat, cook the vinegar until reduced to a syrup. Remove, let cool, and reserve in an airtight container. May be refrigerated for up to 1 week.

FOR THE SHORT RIBS:

2 tablespoons canola oil
Kosher salt
Freshly ground black pepper
3 pounds beef short ribs, cut into 3-inch
    pieces and trimmed of excess fat
    (the butcher can do this)
All-purpose flour
2 large Spanish onions, quartered
2 bulbs fennel, halved
5 cloves garlic, peeled

1/2 (750-milliliter) bottle Cabernet, or
    substitute a quality red wine such as
    Zinfandel or Shiraz
6 cups chicken stock or canned low-sodium
    chicken broth
1 (24-ounce) can plum tomatoes, with
    their juice
3 bay leaves
1 teaspoon red pepper flakes

1. In a large pot, heat the canola oil over medium heat. Lightly salt and pepper the short ribs and roll them in flour, shaking off the excess. Put the ribs in the pot and brown on all sides; remove from the pot.

2. Pour off any excess fat and add the onions, fennel, and garlic cloves to the pot. Cook, stirring frequently to deglaze the beef flavors from the bottom, and to give a bit of color to the vegetables, about 5 minutes.

3. Add the wine and boil gently for 5 minutes, until the alcohol has cooked off. Add the chicken stock and tomatoes and combine well. Return the ribs to the pot and evenly distribute them.

4. Add the bay leaves and red pepper flakes. Taste and season with salt and pepper. Bring the mixture to a boil, cover, and reduce the heat to low. Keep the heat low so that the liquid doesn't reduce too quickly. Simmer until the ribs are fork-tender and falling off the bone, about 1 hour and 20 minutes. (Begin by cooking the ribs for 1 hour, then check every 10 minutes for doneness.)

5. Let the pot stand off the heat for an additional 20 minutes; remove the ribs to a platter and let cool. Hand-shred the meat, remove the fat, and reserve the cooking liquid. The meat and juices can be refrigerated for up to 3 days.

FOR THE POTATOES:

2 pounds Yukon Gold potatoes, unpeeled,
    cut into 1/8-inch dice

Kosher salt

Put the potatoes in a large saucepan and cover with cold water. Add 1 tablespoon salt and bring to a boil over high heat. The potatoes should be done at this point; if they are not, reduce the heat to medium and cook at a gentle boil until fork-tender. Drain, place on a plate or tray, and let cool in the refrigerator. The potatoes can be refrigerated for up to 1 day.

1 tablespoon canola oil, plus more, as needed

1 teaspoon finely chopped garlic, plus more,
    as needed

1 bunch of kale, washed and cut into
    1/2-inch-thin ribbons

1 to 2 tablespoons unsalted butter

6 large eggs

Kosher salt

Freshly ground black pepper

2 scallions (white and 3 inches of green),
    thinly sliced

1. Heat 1 tablespoon canola oil in a large sauté pan over medium-high heat. Add 1 teaspoon chopped garlic and lightly brown. Add 1 cup of cut kale and sauté until softened. Add 1 cup of the cooked potatoes and 1 cup of the shredded beef, and mix well. Add 1/8 cup of the reserved beef-cooking liquid, cook until the mixture is slightly thickened, and remove to a bowl or plate. Repeat until all the kale, potatoes, and beef have been cooked. Return all the ingredients to the pan and reheat briefly.

2. Meanwhile, in a large, preferably nonstick, skillet over medium heat, melt the butter. Break the eggs into the skillet, sprinkle with salt and pepper, cover, and cook until set, 4 to 6 minutes.

TO SERVE, transfer the hash to a large serving platter. Top with the sunny-side-up eggs, and drizzle with balsamic syrup. Sprinkle with the sliced scallions.

Roasted Beef Shanks with Vegetables and Potatoes

Makes 4 to 6 servings

Food commentator and cookbook author Arthur Schwartz was inspired to create this oven-cooked dish when he caramelized some meaty beef shanks, along with vegetables, to make brown stock. He praises this meat for its deep flavor and the richly textured sauce it produces, both ideally suited to the chunky potatoes (peeled or not—it's your call) that complete the dish. Serve this with plenty of crusty bread to soak up the delicious sauce.

4 to 6 (1-inch-thick) slices of beef shank
   (about 3 1/2 pounds total)
Kosher salt
Freshly ground black pepper
8 carrots
8 small onions
2 or 3 parsnips, peeled, tips cut off,
   and heavier tops halved
2 tablespoons olive oil
16 cloves garlic, peeled

1 (14 1/2-ounce) can regular or low-sodium
   beef broth
1 (1-pound) can plum tomatoes, with their
   juice
2 pounds Yukon Gold or Red Bliss potatoes,
   peeled or unpeeled, cut into 2-inch
   chunks
4 fresh parsley sprigs
1/2 teaspoon fresh thyme leaves
1 large bay leaf

1. Preheat the oven to 450°F.

2. In a roasting pan (approximately 15 by 11 inches), arrange the slices of beef shank, preferably without overlapping them. Sprinkle the meat with salt and pepper. Arrange the carrots, onions, and parsnips over and between the pieces of meat. Drizzle on the olive oil. Sprinkle the vegetables with salt and pepper.

3. Place the roasting pan in the oven for 15 minutes. Turn the meat over and rearrange the vegetables. Cook for another 15 minutes, or until the meat is brown. Remove the roasting pan and reduce the oven temperature to 350°F.

4. Add all the remaining ingredients to the pan, breaking up the tomatoes slightly with the side of a wooden spoon. Cover with heavy-duty foil and return to the oven for 1 1/2 to 2 hours, until the meat and vegetables are very tender. The dish may be served with the juices as they are, or the juices may be reduced (see step 5).

5. If you prefer a thicker sauce, remove the meat and all the vegetables except the garlic to a platter; cover with foil to keep warm. Strain the juices into a saucepan, pushing through any tomato bits and the pulp from the garlic. Skim off the surface fat. Place over high heat and reduce the juices slightly, stirring frequently. Pour the thickened juices over the meat and vegetables.

TO SERVE, divide the meat and vegetables, with the sauce, among 4 to 6 deep plates or shallow bowls.

Shepherd's Pie of Beef Shank Braised in Zinfandel

Makes 8 servings

Chef Meer, of Manhattan's City Hall Restaurant, chooses a meaty beef shank when he prepares his shepherd's pie, braising it in Zinfandel and topping it with cheese-spiked mashed potatoes. For perfect potatoes, he urges us never to allow the potatoes to boil, but to simmer them slowly until done, and to be sure the potatoes and the milk are hot when we mix them together.

This cut provides the bonus of rich beef marrow—try it spread on a garlicky toasted baguette.

FOR THE ZINFANDEL-BRAISED BEEF SHANK:

1 beef shank (about 6 pounds)
Kosher salt
Freshly ground black pepper
5 to 6 tablespoons canola oil
6 carrots, cut into medium dice
2 onions, cut into medium dice

1 bunch of celery, cut into medium dice
1 head garlic, unpeeled, halved crosswise
2 bay leaves
1 (750-milliliter) bottle Zinfandel
4 cups water

1. Preheat the oven to 375°F.
2. Season the beef shank well with salt and pepper. In a large casserole over medium-high heat, heat the oil until very hot and sear the beef until browned, 3 to 4 minutes on each side. Cover the casserole tightly with foil and put it in the oven for 45 minutes.
3. Reduce the oven temperature to 300°F.

4. Remove the shank to a plate and skim off any excess fat from the cooking juices. Add the carrots, onions, celery, garlic, and bay leaves to the juices in the casserole and cook over medium-high heat for 12 to 15 minutes. Add the Zinfandel and cook until the liquid is reduced by half, about 30 minutes. Add the water and beef shank, cover tightly with foil and the lid, and return to the oven. Cook for 2 hours.

5. Remove the beef shank and vegetables and allow the meat to cool to room temperature. Remove the meat from the bone, discarding the excess fat and reserving the bone (see Note). Cut the meat into bite-sized cubes.

6. Remove and discard the bay leaves and garlic from the cooking juices. Return the meat to the casserole with the vegetables and add about 2 cups of the cooking juices, just enough to cover the meat. (There will be more liquid than you need. You can reduce the juices over medium-high heat until thickened, or you can reserve the extra liquid for other uses.) The meat can be refrigerated for up to 2 days; reheat when ready to finish the recipe.

FOR THE MASHED-POTATO TOPPING:

3 pounds Yukon Gold potatoes, peeled
    and cut into large chunks
Kosher salt
1 to 1 1/2 cups milk
4 1/2 tablespoons unsalted butter, at room
    temperature

8 ounces Parmigiano-Reggiano cheese,
    freshly grated
Freshly ground black pepper

1. Put the potatoes in a large pot and cover with cold water. Add 1 tablespoon salt and bring to a simmer over medium-high heat. Simmer until tender, 25 to 30 minutes.

2. While the potatoes are cooking, heat the milk in a small pot over medium heat.

3. Drain the potatoes, put them in a large bowl, and mash with a potato masher until smooth. With a wooden spoon, mix in the butter, then mix in the warm milk. Add the Parmigiano-Reggiano cheese and combine well. Season with salt and pepper.

TO MAKE THE SHEPHERD'S PIE:

1. Preheat the oven to 350°F.

2. Spoon the mashed potatoes over the meat-and-vegetable mixture in the casserole. Place in the oven for about 30 minutes, or until the potatoes are browned and the meat mixture is bubbling. Serve from the casserole.

NOTE: You can enjoy the marrow from the shank bone along with the shepherd's pie. Stand the reserved shank bone on end and split it down the middle with a cleaver. Spoon out the marrow. Halve a baguette lengthwise and toast it. Rub 1 clove of garlic over the surface of the bread and spread with the roasted marrow. Season with salt and pepper to taste.

If you have refrigerated the cooked bone, before splitting, reheat it in a 300°F oven for 10 minutes.

BEEF

Shepherd's Pie of Merlot-Braised Oxtail

Makes 4 to 6 servings

Oxtail requires long, slow braising to unlock its deep flavor and tenderness. But be generous with your time, and the result will be unusually rich and satisfying. Infused with earthy wild mushrooms, topped with creamy truffled mashed potatoes, and perfumed with black truffle, Chef Sundstrom's dish from Seattle's Earth and Ocean is a knockout.

FOR THE MERLOT-BRAISED OXTAILS:

2 carrots, diced

1 onion, diced

2 stalks celery, diced

1 head garlic, cloves crushed with the broad
    end of a knife blade and peeled

2 bay leaves

1 tablespoon black peppercorns

2 cups Merlot

3 to 4 pounds oxtails, cut into chunks and
    trimmed of excess fat

3 tablespoons olive oil

4 cups chicken, veal, or beef stock, or canned
    low-sodium chicken or beef broth

3 tablespoons kosher salt

1. In a large nonreactive bowl, combine the carrots, onion, celery, garlic cloves, bay leaves, peppercorns, and Merlot. Add the oxtails and toss to coat well with the marinade. Cover and refrigerate for 5 hours or up to 24 hours.

2. Remove the oxtails with a slotted spoon or tongs, and separately reserve the meat; the carrots, onion, and celery; and the wine. Pat the meat dry with paper towels.

3. In a large roasting pan over medium-high heat, heat the olive oil until very hot, and brown the oxtails well on all sides. Remove the meat from the pan. Add the reserved

carrots, onion, and celery and cook for 15 minutes. Add the reserved wine and boil gently until the alcohol has cooked off, about 5 minutes.

4. Return the oxtails to the pan and add the stock. Sprinkle well with the salt. Increase the heat to high, and bring to a boil. Reduce the heat to low, cover, and simmer on the stovetop until the meat is very tender and beginning to fall off the bone, 3 to 3$\frac{1}{2}$ hours. (Or place the covered pan in a preheated 300°F oven for 3 to 3$\frac{1}{2}$ hours.)

5. Remove the meat and set it aside to cool. Pour the contents of the roasting pan into a strainer set over a large pot and discard the vegetables. Skim any fat from the braising liquid, then gently simmer over medium-low heat until slightly thickened and concentrated. Reserve. Remove the oxtail meat from the bones and reserve.

FOR THE RAGOUT:

1 tablespoon unsalted butter
1 cup combined red and white pearl onions,
    or substitute all white pearl onions
    (or use frozen pearl onions)
1 teaspoon minced garlic
2 cups combined assorted wild (and/or domestic) mushrooms (such as porcini, morels, chanterelles, cremini, and shiitakes), cut or torn into bite-sized pieces

$\frac{1}{2}$ cup Merlot
Kosher or sea salt
Freshly ground black pepper

1. In a large sauté pan over medium heat, melt the butter, and sauté the pearl onions until tender. Add the garlic and mushrooms, and sauté until the garlic is just golden.

2. Add the Merlot and simmer until reduced by half. Add the oxtail meat and 1 cup of the braising liquid. Simmer until the vegetables are well coated and the sauce is reduced

by half; adjust the seasoning. The ragout can be refrigerated for up to 3 days; reheat before continuing with the recipe.

FOR THE TRUFFLED-MASHED-POTATO TOPPING:

3 Yukon Gold potatoes, peeled and cut into
    large dice
Kosher or sea salt
1 cup heavy cream
8 tablespoons unsalted butter, cut into
    small pieces

1 ounce black truffle, thinly sliced or shaved
    (see Sources)
Freshly ground white pepper

1. Cover the potatoes with cold water in a large saucepan, add 1 tablespoon salt, and simmer over medium heat until tender. Drain, then pass through a fine-mesh sieve, food mill, or ricer into a large bowl.

2. Mix in the cream, butter, and truffle. Season with salt and white pepper.

TO MAKE THE SHEPHERD'S PIES:

1/2 cup freshly grated Parmesan cheese

1. Preheat the oven to 400°F or preheat the broiler.

2. Divide the oxtail ragout among 4 to 6 individual casserole dishes set on a sheet pan and press the mixture down. Top each with truffled mashed potatoes, press down again, and smooth the tops. Sprinkle with the grated Parmesan cheese. Bake or broil until

the tops are light golden and the pies are heated through. (The mixture can also be baked in a 9 by 9-inch casserole.)

3. Meanwhile, in a small saucepan over medium heat, simmer the reserved braising liquid until slightly reduced.

4. Place the individual casseroles on serving plates and drizzle with the warmed braising liquid.

Braised Beef Cheeks with Fingerling Potato Purée

BEEF

Makes 4 servings

The unusually delicious and silky cut of beef blends perfectly with a buttery purée of fingerlings, in this recipe from Chef Renaud of Manhattan's Fleur de Sel. The combination is rich and memorable. Should there be any leftovers, they will be even better the next day.

Beef cheeks are not always easy to find at your neighborhood butcher, but widen your search—they are worth it.

FOR THE BRAISED BEEF CHEEKS:

1 (750-milliliter) bottle Malbec, or substitute
 Merlot or Cabernet
2 pounds beef cheeks, cut into 16 pieces,
 trimmed of excess fat but some fat left
 for flavor (see Sources; or substitute beef
 round or veal shank)
Kosher salt
Freshly ground black pepper

1/2 cup canola oil
6 shallots, thinly sliced
1 head garlic, cloves peeled and roughly
 chopped
8 cups veal stock, or substitute canned
 low-sodium beef broth combined with
 4 ounces tomato paste

1. In a medium saucepan over medium-high heat, bring the wine to a boil. Cook at a low boil until the wine is reduced by half.

2. Preheat the oven to 450°F.

3. Season the beef cheeks on all sides with salt and pepper.

4. In a large ovenproof saucepan, heat the canola oil over medium-high heat until it smokes slightly. Add the beef cheeks, fat side down, and cook, turning to brown them on all sides. Remove the meat from the pan.

5. Reduce the heat to medium and add the shallots and garlic to the pan. Season with salt and pepper, and cook until the shallots are softened and translucent but not colored, about 10 minutes. Return the meat to the pan, add the reduced wine and the veal stock, and bring to a boil, skimming off any scum that forms.

6. Cover with foil or a lid and place in the oven for about 2 hours, or until the beef is fork-tender. Pour the contents of the pan into a colander set over a large bowl and separate the meat and the sauce. Brush off any garlic or shallots that remain on the meat.

7. Pour the sauce through a fine-mesh strainer into a saucepan, and place over medium-high heat. Simmer until the sauce is reduced by about two-thirds or it is thick enough to coat the back of a spoon. Season with salt and pepper, and combine with the meat. Keep warm until ready to serve.

FOR THE FINGERLING POTATO PURÉE:

2¹/2 pounds fingerling potatoes, peeled (or substitute Red Bliss)
Kosher salt
1¹/4 pounds (5 sticks) unsalted butter, cut into small pieces

1¹/2 cups whole milk
3/4 cup heavy cream
Freshly ground black pepper

1. Put the potatoes in a large pot and cover with cold water. Add 1 tablespoon salt and bring to a simmer over medium-high heat. Simmer until the potatoes are fork-tender, about 35 minutes. Drain the potatoes and pass them through a food mill or ricer into a mixing bowl. Mix in the butter.

2. Warm the milk and cream in a small saucepan over medium heat. Add half to the potato mixture, stirring until it is absorbed. Continue adding and stirring until the purée is smooth; you may not need all the liquid. Season with salt and pepper.

TO SERVE, divide the meat and sauce among 4 plates, and spoon the potato purée alongside.

Provençal Bouilli (Boiled Beef and Vegetables)

Makes 6 servings

Chef Antoine Bouterin, of Manhattan's Bouterin Restaurant, remembers how his mother prepared this fragrant stew on cool days in Saint-Rémy-de-Provence when he was a child. She would let it cook gently all afternoon, so the flavors of the meat and farm-fresh vegetables melted into one another. It was—and is—a perfect family meal.

FOR THE BOUQUET GARNI:

3 flat-leaf parsley sprigs
2 fresh basil sprigs

2 fresh thyme sprigs
2 bay leaves

Wrap the parsley, basil, thyme, and bay leaves in a small square of cheesecloth. Tie with string, if necessary, to hold the package together.

3 pounds beef chuck, or substitute rump

2 large onions, 1 stuck with 4 cloves and
    1 halved

1 tablespoon kosher salt

1 tablespoon black peppercorns

3 large carrots

3 large leeks (white and tender green parts),
    washed

2 cloves garlic, unpeeled, crushed with the
    broad end of a knife blade

2 small turnips, peeled and quartered

3 stalks celery

1 large tomato, halved

2 small parsnips, peeled and thickly sliced

10 small potatoes (such as Red Bliss),
    unpeeled

1 small cabbage, quartered

6 allspice berries

1. Put the meat in a large pot and cover with water by 4 inches. Add the bouquet garni, onions, salt, and peppercorns and bring to a boil over high heat. Add the carrots, leeks, garlic, turnips, celery, and tomato. Reduce the heat to medium and boil gently, uncovered, for about 3 hours. Skim occasionally.

2. Add the parsnips, potatoes, cabbage, and allspice berries, and simmer until the potatoes and parsnips are tender, about 30 minutes. Strain the broth, reserving the meat and vegetables. Discard the bouquet garni, peppercorns, and cloves.

TO SERVE, slice the meat about 1/4 inch thick and return it to the broth, with the vegetables. Serve as a main-course soup, in large bowls; or serve the broth as a first course and the meat and vegetables as a main course.

Boeuf Bourguignon

Makes 4 to 6 servings

Manhattan's Levana Restaurant is the source for this sophisticated yet simple stew. Preparation is a snap, but the deep flavors of the meat, vegetables, and herbs make the result extraordinary. This dish reheats very well, and improves after a day or two, making it perfect for a do-ahead dinner party. As a kosher cook, Levana uses meat that has been pre-salted, so her original recipe doesn't call for any additional salt. We have added some to the recipe for cooks who use unsalted meat.

3 tablespoons extra-virgin olive oil

3 pounds beef shoulder, cut into 2-inch cubes

6 cloves garlic, peeled

2 cups dry red wine

2 large tomatoes, cut into small dice

Kosher salt

1 tablespoon freshly ground black pepper

6 bay leaves

4 fresh thyme sprigs, leaves only

2 pounds very thin carrots (about 20)

20 very small potatoes, unpeeled

12 small onions

1. To cook in a Crock-Pot, layer the oil, beef, garlic cloves, wine, and tomatoes in a 6-quart Crock-Pot, seasoning each layer lightly with salt and pepper. Top with the bay leaves, thyme, carrots, potatoes, and onions. Set the Crock-Pot on low and cook for 10 to 12 hours.

2. To cook on the stovetop, place the oil, beef, and 8 cups of water in a wide, heavy pot over high heat and bring to a boil. Reduce the heat to medium and cook, covered, for 2 hours. Add the garlic, wine, tomatoes, salt, pepper, and bay leaves and cook for an addi-

tional 30 minutes. Add the thyme, carrots, potatoes, and onions, season to taste, and cook for another 30 minutes. The meat should be fork-tender.

3. Using a slotted spoon, transfer the meat and vegetables to a serving platter. If the liquid left in the pot is too thin, reduce it over high heat until it is thickened to the consistency of maple syrup. Pour the reduced liquid over the meat and vegetables, and serve hot.

BEEF

Malaysian Beef Rendang with Sweet Potato–Coconut Purée

Makes 4 to 6 servings

Chef Yeo presents meat and potatoes in a brilliant and unexpected form in this Malaysian dish that she remembers as a childhood favorite. Rendang combines the complex notes of coconut and chilies and is served with a sweet potato purée that repeats and intensifies the coconut flavor.

FOR THE BEEF RENDANG:

1 pound shredded unsweetened dried coconut

10 assorted dried chilies (such as Thai bird, guajillo, and ancho), soaked for at least 2 hours or overnight, drained, seeded, and stemmed (see Sources)

4 cups coarsely chopped shallots

2 1/2 pounds beef stew meat (such as chuck), cut into 1-inch pieces

2 kaffir lime leaves (see Sources)

2 stalks lemongrass, tough ends trimmed off, tender stalks cut into 3-inch pieces and crushed (see Sources)

2 (2-inch) pieces of galangal (see Sources; or substitute fresh ginger)

5 cups unsweetened coconut milk

Kosher salt

Freshly ground black pepper

1. Preheat the oven to 325°F.

2. Spread the coconut out on a large sheet pan and toast, stirring every 8 to 10 minutes, for about 25 minutes, or until golden and fragrant.

3. In a food processor, combine 2 tablespoons of the toasted coconut with the soaked chilies and the shallots. Process to a paste and transfer to a large, heavy pot.

4. Add the beef and toss to coat well. Place the pot over medium-high heat, add the remaining ingredients, and bring to a boil. Reduce the heat to a simmer and cook, stirring occasionally, until the meat is tender, about 30 minutes.

5. Increase the heat to medium-high and cook the rendang, stirring constantly, until the coconut oil starts to separate from the sauce and the sauce is thick and fairly dry (this may take up to 30 minutes). The coconut will be browned and toasty, and the dish will be dry and not too saucy. Taste and adjust the salt and pepper.

FOR THE SWEET POTATO-COCONUT PURÉE:

1 (14-ounce) can unsweetened coconut milk
6 large sweet potatoes, peeled and cut into
    large chunks

Kosher salt
Freshly grated nutmeg
Freshly ground black pepper

1. In a saucepan over medium-high heat, simmer the coconut milk until reduced by one-quarter.

2. Meanwhile, boil the sweet potatoes in a large pot of lightly salted water until very tender. Drain well and transfer to a food processor or mixer. Add the reduced coconut milk and a few gratings of nutmeg and pulse together just until smooth. Season to taste with additional nutmeg, salt, and pepper, and serve hot.

SERVE   the beef rendang with the sweet potato–coconut purée.

BEEF

Meat Loaf Stuffed with Mashed Potatoes and Cheddar

Makes 4 to 6 servings

Everyone loves savory meat loaf served with fluffy mashed potatoes, and Chef Kenney combines the two favorites in a single dish—accented with Cheddar cheese. As the potatoes cook, they are flavored with the meat's juices and the melting cheese, and each generous slice of meat loaf offers layers of color and texture.

FOR THE MASHED POTATOES:

1 pound russet potatoes, unpeeled
Kosher salt
1 tablespoon unsalted butter, at room
* temperature*

¹/₄ cup light cream or milk
Freshly ground black pepper

1. Put the potatoes in a medium pot and cover with cold water. Add 1 tablespoon salt and bring to a simmer over medium-high heat. Cook until the potatoes are tender, 25 to 30 minutes.

2. Drain, peel, and quarter the potatoes. In a mixing bowl, mash them coarsely with a potato masher or fork, blending in the butter. Mix in the cream, as needed. Season with salt and pepper. Small pieces of potato are fine; this should not be a purée.

Olive oil
1 pound ground beef chuck
3/4 cup plain bread crumbs
1 small onion, finely chopped
3 cloves garlic, minced
1/3 cup ketchup

1 large egg, lightly beaten
1 teaspoon Tabasco sauce
1 teaspoon kosher salt
1/2 teaspoon freshly ground black pepper
2 to 3 ounces Cheddar cheese, thinly sliced

1. Preheat the oven to 400°F. Lightly oil a large loaf pan or a high-sided sheet pan.

2. In a large mixing bowl, combine the ground beef, bread crumbs, onion, garlic, ketchup, egg, Tabasco, salt, and pepper.

3. On a sheet of foil, pat out the meat into a square of approximately 10 by 10 inches. Arrange the cheese slices over the meat, leaving a narrow border all around. Spoon the mashed potatoes in an even layer over the cheese. Using the foil as a guide, fold one side of the meat up over the other, and press down all around to seal. Gently form the meat into a loaf shape.

4. Place the meat loaf in the prepared pan, seam side down, and brush the top lightly with olive oil. Bake for about 45 minutes, or until cooked through. Cut into thick slices to serve.

Crispy Meat Loaf with Chanterelle-Buttermilk Gravy and Potato Gratin

Makes 8 servings

Bubby's Pie Company, in Tribeca, is famous for this crisp-topped home-style meat loaf, served alongside the easiest gratin I've ever encountered—and one of the best. But it is Chef Crismon's mushroom gravy that puts the dish over the top. It is fragrant with golden chanterelles, garlic, and herbs, and smoothed with a combination of buttermilk and rich cream.

FOR THE CRISPY MEAT LOAF:

1 tablespoon unsalted butter
1 yellow onion, thinly sliced
1 clove garlic, chopped
1 teaspoon chopped fresh tarragon
1/4 cup freshly grated Parmesan cheese
1 teaspoon chopped fresh thyme

1 1/4 cups cornflake crumbs
3/4 cup ketchup
2 large eggs
2 pounds ground beef chuck
1 teaspoon salt
1/2 teaspoon freshly ground black pepper

1. Preheat the oven to 375°F. (If you are not making the potato gratin at the same time, preheat the oven to 400°F.)

2. In a medium skillet, melt the butter over medium heat. Add the onion and reduce the heat to medium-low. Cook, stirring, until the onion softens and then gradually turns a golden caramel color, about 25 minutes.

3. In a large bowl, combine the caramelized onion with the garlic, tarragon, Parmesan cheese, thyme, 1 cup of the cornflake crumbs, 1/2 cup of the ketchup, the eggs, ground beef, salt, and pepper. Mix thoroughly.

4. On a sheet of parchment paper or foil, shape the meat into a loaf; or form it in a large loaf pan. Brush with the remaining 1/4 cup ketchup, then sprinkle with the remaining 1/4 cup cornflake crumbs. Bake in a loaf pan or in a high-sided sheet pan for 40 to 45 minutes, until browned.

FOR THE POTATO GRATIN:

Unsalted butter

2 pounds russet potatoes, peeled, sliced 1/8 inch thick, and put into a bowl of cold water

1 yellow onion, halved lengthwise and thinly sliced

1 cup heavy cream

Pinch of ground nutmeg

Pinch of ground cloves

1/4 teaspoon ground cinnamon

6 ounces Cheddar cheese, freshly grated

6 ounces Parmesan cheese, freshly grated

Kosher salt

Freshly ground black pepper

1. Preheat the oven to 375°F. Lightly butter a 12 by 8-inch baking pan.

2. Drain the potatoes and dry them with paper towels. Put them in a mixing bowl and add the onion, cream, nutmeg, cloves, cinnamon, 4 ounces of the grated Cheddar cheese, 4 ounces of the grated Parmesan cheese, and salt and pepper to taste. Combine well and pour into the prepared baking pan. Top with the remaining 2 ounces Cheddar and 2 ounces Parmesan, and bake for 45 to 50 minutes, until the potatoes are soft and the top is golden brown.

3 tablespoons unsalted butter

1 tablespoon finely diced red onion

1/2 clove garlic, finely chopped

8 ounces chanterelle mushrooms, thickly sliced

2 tablespoons all-purpose flour

2 cups chicken stock or canned low-sodium
    chicken broth

1 tablespoon chopped fresh thyme

1/2 cup heavy cream

1/2 cup buttermilk

Kosher salt

Freshly ground black pepper

2 tablespoons chopped fresh parsley

1. In a large saucepan over medium-high heat, melt the butter. Add the onion and garlic and sauté until sizzling. Add the mushrooms and cook, stirring, until softened. Add the flour and mix until smooth. Cook, stirring frequently, for 4 minutes.

2. Add the chicken stock and stir constantly for 1 to 2 minutes. Add the thyme, reduce the heat to low, and simmer for 20 minutes. Add the cream and buttermilk, season with salt and pepper, and simmer, stirring occasionally, for 8 to 10 minutes. Stir in the parsley.

TO SERVE, cut the meat loaf into thick slices and divide among 8 plates. Spoon the gratin alongside the meat loaf, and pass the gravy separately.

DIANA BARRIOS TREVIÑO

Chiles Rellenos with Warm Mild Tomato Sauce

Makes 8 servings

Chef Barrios Treviño presides over San Antonio's famous Los Barrios Restaurant, the place to go for authentic Tex-Mex cuisine. In her take on this classic dish, poblanos are stuffed with a spicy mixture of meat and potatoes, dipped in flour and egg, and fried until golden. Serve them under a mantle of fresh tomato sauce that mellows their heat.

FOR THE WARM MILD TOMATO SAUCE:

4 tomatoes, quartered
1/4 cup vegetable oil
1 onion, thinly sliced
1/2 green bell pepper, thinly sliced

1/4 teaspoon garlic powder
1/8 teaspoon ground cumin
1/2 teaspoon kosher salt
1/4 teaspoon freshly ground black pepper

1. Put the tomatoes in a blender and blend until puréed.
2. In a medium skillet, heat the oil over medium heat and cook the onion and bell pepper until soft, 3 to 5 minutes. Add the puréed tomatoes, garlic powder, cumin, salt, and pepper and bring to a simmer. Reduce the heat to low and simmer gently for about 45 minutes.

BEEF

1/4 cup olive oil
2 pounds ground beef chuck
1/2 teaspoon kosher salt
1/2 teaspoon freshly ground black pepper
1/2 teaspoon garlic powder
1/2 teaspoon ground cumin
1 russet potato, peeled and diced

1 carrot, diced
8 roasted and peeled poblano chilies
   (see Note)
5 large eggs, separated and yolks beaten
All-purpose flour
Vegetable oil

1. In a large skillet, heat the olive oil over medium heat and add the ground beef. Season with the salt, pepper, garlic powder, and cumin, and cook, stirring to break up any lumps, until the meat is browned, 6 to 8 minutes. Add the potato and carrot and cook, stirring occasionally, until they are fork-tender, 8 to 10 minutes. Remove from the heat.

2. Make a slit down the side of each peeled poblano chili and remove the seeds. Stuff the chiles with the meat mixture.

3. In a large bowl, beat the egg whites until they form stiff peaks. Beat in the egg yolks.

4. Spread the flour on a sheet of waxed paper.

5. Pour 1 inch of vegetable oil into a large, deep skillet and heat until very hot. One at a time, roll the stuffed peppers in the flour to coat, then dip into the egg mixture and add to the pan. Cook one at a time until lightly browned on one side, 30 to 60 seconds. Turn and brown on the second side. Remove with a slotted spoon and drain briefly on paper towels.

TO SERVE, place the stuffed chiles on a platter and top with the tomato sauce.

NOTE: To roast poblano chilies, preheat the oven to 350°F. Lightly brush the chilies with vegetable oil and place on a cookie sheet. Roast, turning the chilies every 10 minutes, for about 30 minutes, or until the skin begins to split and peel. Put the chilies in a plastic bag, seal the bag, and let the chilies sit until they are cool enough to handle. Then peel off the skin.

BEEF

Potato Gnocchi with Ragù Bolognese

Makes 4 main-course or 6 first-course servings

Inspired by a recent trip through Italy, Keith Dresser, of *Cook's Illustrated* magazine, created this robust Mediterranean-style meat-and-potato combination. The meaty, long-simmered sauce marries perfectly with the flavor and texture of light, chewy potato gnocchi. Keith advises that while homemade gnocchi are the best by far, you can substitute a good-quality prepared product, if necessary.

FOR THE RAGÙ BOLOGNESE:

2 tablespoons tomato paste
3/4 cup chicken stock or low-sodium canned
    chicken broth
2 tablespoons extra-virgin olive oil
2 ounces pancetta, finely chopped
1 1/2 pounds coarsely ground beef chuck

1 large carrot, finely chopped
2 small stalks celery, finely chopped
1/2 onion, finely chopped
1/2 cup dry white wine
1 1/2 cups whole milk

1. Combine the tomato paste and chicken stock, and set aside.

2. Put the olive oil and pancetta in a Dutch oven over medium heat and cook until the pancetta has rendered most of its fat, about 7 minutes.

3. Raise the heat to medium-high, add the beef, and cook, stirring frequently, until the beef is well browned, 8 to 10 minutes. Stir in the carrot, celery, and onion, and sauté until the onion is translucent, about 3 minutes.

4. Stir in the wine and diluted tomato paste. Reduce the heat to low and simmer for 10 minutes. Stir in $1/2$ cup of the milk and simmer for 25 minutes. Repeat the process of adding $1/2$ cup of the milk and simmering for 25 minutes two more times, until all the milk is used and the sauce is the consistency of a thick soup.

FOR THE POTATO GNOCCHI:

$1^1/2$ pounds russet potatoes, unpeeled

1 cup all-purpose flour, plus more as needed

$1^1/2$ teaspoons kosher salt

1. Preheat the oven to 400°F.

2. Bake the potatoes for about 1 hour, or until a thin-bladed paring knife slides in without resistance.

3. While the potatoes are still hot, peel them with a paring knife. Pass the potatoes through a food mill or ricer into a large bowl. Let the potatoes cool slightly, about 10 minutes.

4. Sprinkle the flour and salt over the potatoes. Mix with a wooden spoon until a soft, smooth dough has formed. If the mixture is sticky, add more flour as needed, 1 tablespoon at a time.

5. Divide the dough into 4 equal pieces. Roll each piece of dough into a 1-inch-thick rope (if the dough breaks apart while rolling, put it back into the bowl and add more flour).

6. Sprinkle a tray or sheet pan lightly with flour. Cut each rope into 1-inch pieces. Holding a fork in one hand and a 1-inch dough piece in the other, gently press and roll the dough against the fork tines, and flick the gnocchi off the tines onto the lightly floured tray. Each piece of gnocchi should have a slight indentation on one side, from your finger, and grooves on the other, from the fork. The gnocchi can be refrigerated for up to 2 hours or frozen for up to 1 month.

Kosher salt
1/2 cup freshly grated Parmesan cheese, or to
 taste

Bring 6 quarts of water to a boil in a large pot. Add 1 tablespoon of kosher salt. Add half of the gnocchi and cook until they float to the surface, 1 1/2 to 2 minutes. Remove the gnocchi from the water with a slotted spoon and place in a warmed serving dish or in individual bowls. Repeat with the remaining gnocchi. Top with the *ragù,* sprinkle with the Parmesan cheese, and serve immediately.

3.

Veal, Mixed Meats, and Potatoes

*T*HIS SHORT LIST CAPTURES THE VERSATILITY OF VEAL AND ITS COMPATABILITY WITH different preparations—and several types of potatoes. Sweet, russet, Yukon Gold, and German Butterball potatoes complement this subtle, delicate meat in a variety of dishes.

Laurent Gras pairs lean, sautéed tournedos of veal with potatoes cooked two ways: caramelized and creamy. He tops this complex mix of textures with fruity, sweet sautéed apple slices, in a virtuoso dish. Country-Style Veal Chops with Potatoes and Mushrooms, from my kitchen, is a version of a traditional farm supper, easy to cook, tender, and wonderfully fragrant.

Allen Susser roasts a rack of juicy veal and accompanies it with pancakes that combine grated potatoes (familiar) with roasted red bell peppers (unexpected). Adding another surprise, he crusts the veal roast with crisp celery seeds.

Walter Potenza gently cooks veal shoulder in a tangy, herbaceous tomato sauce with eggplant and zucchini and bakes it with feathery potato gnocchi, under a mantle of melting Pecorino Romano cheese. Gerry Hayden works magic with Slow-Braised Veal and Vanilla Sweet Potato Shepherd's Pie, combining sweet and savory flavors with tender braised veal breast.

I love the light yet chewy texture of ground veal, and in my Veal Croquettes with Dilled New Potatoes, it is highlighted by a bit of cream. Fresh dill, tossed with buttery potatoes, is the perfect herbal accent.

If one tender, delicious cut of meat is good, three must be better! Two unusual dishes are enriched by a mixture of several meats: Philippe Bertineau's Baeckeofe, a meat-and-potato casserole from Alsace, combines chunks of beef, lamb, and pork with potatoes, for traditional slow baking; and Carla Pellegrino's La Svizzera with Prosciutto Mashed Potatoes, a sophisticated yet home-style Italian burger, puts ground beef, veal, and pork to excellent use.

Veal Tournedos with Caramelized and Creamy Potatoes and Sautéed Apple Slices

Makes 4 servings

Adapted from Chef Gras's elegant creation, served at San Francisco's Fifth Floor Restaurant, this version of veal tournedos is somewhat simpler than the original but is based on his classic yet imaginative concept. Delicate veal tournedos are joined with potatoes done two ways—creamy and caramelized—and sweetened by golden sautéed apple slices. The combination equals pure poetry!

FOR THE CREAMY POTATOES:

3/4 cup chicken stock or canned low-sodium
    chicken broth
2 pounds German Butterball potatoes,
    unpeeled (see Sources; or substitute
    Yukon Gold)

Kosher salt
8 tablespoons (1 stick) unsalted butter
1 flat-leaf parsley sprig, roughly chopped

1. In a small saucepan over high heat, bring the stock to a boil. Remove from the heat and reserve.

2. Put the potatoes in a pot large enough to accommodate them and cover with lightly salted cold water. Bring to a simmer and cook over medium-high heat until fork-tender, about 30 minutes, depending on the size of the potatoes.

3. Drain and peel the potatoes and pass them through a food mill or ricer into a large pan set over low heat. Add the reserved chicken stock and 4 tablespoons of the butter, and

mix well. Stir in the remaining 4 tablespoons butter and season with salt. Just before serving, stir in the chopped parsley.

FOR THE CARAMELIZED POTATOES:

4 russet or Yukon Gold potatoes, peeled and
    sliced lengthwise about 1/2 inch thick
    (there should be about 8 pieces)
2 tablespoons clarified unsalted butter
    (see Notes)

1/2 cup veal stock, or substitute beef stock
    or canned low-sodium beef broth
Fleur de sel or other sea salt, or substitute
    kosher salt
Freshly ground black pepper

In a large skillet over medium-high heat, sauté the potato slices in the clarified butter until golden, 4 to 5 minutes on each side. Add the stock (be careful that it doesn't splatter) and cook until the stock is reduced and the potatoes are caramelized, another 4 to 5 minutes. Sprinkle with fleur de sel and pepper.

FOR THE SAUTÉED APPLE SLICES:

1 Golden Delicious apple, peeled, halved, and
    sliced 1/4 inch thick (there should be
    about 16 slices)
1 tablespoon clarified unsalted butter
    (see Notes)
1 tablespoon demi-glace (see Sources) or veal
    stock, or substitute beef stock or canned
    low-sodium beef broth

Fleur de sel or other sea salt, or substitute
    kosher salt
Freshly cracked black pepper (see Notes)

In a medium skillet over medium heat, sauté the apple slices in the clarified butter until golden and softened, about 10 minutes. Brush with demi-glace (or toss with the stock) and sprinkle with fleur de sel and pepper.

FOR THE VEAL TOURNEDOS:

4 boneless veal loin chops (about 4 ounces each)
Fleur de sel or other sea salt, or substitute kosher salt

Freshly ground black pepper
2 tablespoons canola oil
Demi-glace (see Sources), veal stock, beef stock, or canned low-sodium beef broth

1. Preheat the oven to 300°F.
2. Season the veal chops with fleur de sel and pepper on one side only. In a large skillet over medium-high heat, heat the canola oil until very hot and sear the veal on both sides until golden, 2 to 3 minutes on each side. Place the veal on a baking sheet, brush with the demi-glace, and bake for about 10 minutes, or until cooked through. (Be careful not to overcook and dry out the meat.)

TO SERVE, place one tournedo of veal on the bottom half of each plate and place the caramelized potatoes on the top half. Spoon the creamy potatoes across the center, and arrange the apple slices over all.

NOTES: To clarify butter, melt it over low heat and simmer briefly. Pour off and use the clear yellow portion, and discard the milky solids. You will lose about one-quarter of the butter this way, so start with some extra. Or microwave the butter for 1 to 2 minutes, skim off the foam, and use the clear yellow portion. Discard the milky solids.

For cracked black pepper, wrap peppercorns in a dish towel and smash them with a heavy pan.

Country-Style Veal Chops with Potatoes and Mushrooms

Makes 4 servings

The simplest, best ingredients, combined with the easiest of methods, make this a family favorite. And your kitchen smells heavenly while the veal, potatoes, and mushrooms cook.

4 russet or Yukon Gold potatoes (1¹/₂ to
    2 pounds), unpeeled
¹/₄ cup olive oil, plus extra for the
    baking dish
2 large onions, thinly sliced
4 cloves garlic, crushed with the broad end of a
    knife blade, peeled, and minced

10 ounces domestic white mushrooms, thickly
    sliced
Kosher salt
Freshly ground black pepper
¹/₂ cup chopped flat-leaf parsley
4 rib or loin veal chops, ¹/₂ to ³/₄ inch thick,
    trimmed of excess fat

1. Microwave the potatoes until they are barely cooked through. When they are cool enough to handle, peel and slice 1/2 inch thick.

2. Preheat the oven to 350°F. Lightly oil a baking dish large enough to accommodate the veal chops in one layer.

3. In a large skillet over medium heat, heat 2 tablespoons of the olive oil and cook the onions and garlic until the onions are softened but not colored. Add the mushrooms and cook until softened. Season with salt and pepper and pour into a mixing bowl. Add the parsley and mix well.

4. Season the veal chops with salt and pepper. Add the remaining 2 tablespoons oil to the pan and heat over medium-high heat. Sear the veal chops until browned on both sides, 5 to 6 minutes total. Turn off the heat and leave the chops in the pan.

5. Layer half the potatoes in the baking dish, and season with salt and pepper. Top with all 4 veal chops, reserving the pan juices. Spoon the onion mixture over the chops. Top with the remaining potatoes, and season with salt and pepper. Pour the reserved pan juices over the potatoes.

6. Cover the dish tightly with foil or a lid and bake for about 45 minutes, or until the chops are very tender. Serve from the baking dish.

Celery Seed–Crusted Veal Roast with Red Pepper–Potato Pancakes

Makes 6 servings

Both the tender rack of veal and the crisp potato pancakes—perfect partners—are given a surprising new twist by Allen Susser, of Chef Allen's, in Miami Beach. The roast is crusted with crisp celery seeds, and the pancakes are brightened with juicy chunks of red bell pepper. When you carve this roast, Chef Allen reminds you to reserve the meaty bones, for an especially tasty treat.

FOR THE CELERY SEED–CRUSTED VEAL:

2 tablespoons minced fresh thyme
1 tablespoon minced fresh rosemary
1 tablespoon crushed garlic
1 tablespoon black peppercorns
1 tablespoon kosher salt
2 tablespoons olive oil

1 (5-pound) rack of veal, shoulder blade and
*   flap of meat over the rack removed,*
*   bones trimmed, and the rack tied*
*   so that it will sit better in the pan*
*   (the butcher can do this)*
3 tablespoons celery seeds

1. Preheat the oven to 375°F.

2. In a small bowl, combine the thyme, rosemary, garlic, black peppercorns, salt, and olive oil. Rub the mixture into the veal.

3. Put the veal on a rack in a roasting pan, with the bones down, and place it in the center of the oven. Roast for 30 minutes, then turn the meat over, reduce the heat to 350°F, and roast for another 20 minutes. Remove the veal from the oven and roll it in the celery seeds. Return it to the oven until well browned, about 15 minutes more.

4. Remove the veal from the oven and let it rest for 10 minutes, tented with foil, in a warm spot over the oven, before slicing.

1 large red bell pepper
1 tablespoon olive oil
3 red-skinned potatoes, peeled
1/2 Spanish onion
1 large egg

2 tablespoons matzo meal
Kosher salt
Freshly ground black pepper
1/2 cup peanut oil

1. Rub the red bell pepper with the olive oil and roast it in the oven with the veal until well cooked. Place it in a bowl, cover with a dish towel, and set aside for 15 minutes. Peel, skin, and seed the pepper, then cut the flesh into half-inch dice.

2. Grate the potatoes and onion on a hand grater into a large mixing bowl. Mix in the red pepper, egg, and matzo meal, and season with salt and pepper.

3. In a sauté pan over medium-high heat, heat the peanut oil until shimmering. Drop in the batter by tablespoons, making silver dollar–sized pancakes. Brown the pancakes for about 1 minute on each side, and cook until crisp and cooked through, 3 to 4 minutes more on each side. Reduce the heat to medium if the pancakes are becoming too brown. Drain on paper towels.

4. Place the pancakes on a sheet pan and keep them warm in the oven (reduce the oven temperature to 250°F while the veal is resting).

TO SERVE, slice the meat 1 inch thick and place on individual plates. Place 2 pancakes alongside each serving.

Veal Stew Baked with Gnocchi

VEAL

Makes 4 to 6 servings

Chef Potenza, the Providence restaurateur, cooking teacher, and food historian, recommends that you bake this *tegamata di vitello e gnocchi* in a terra-cotta casserole, for true Italian flavor. The stew is first cooked on the stovetop, and while it is simmering, you can prepare the potato gnocchi. Then combine the meat and potatoes under a sprinkling of grated Romano, and bake. The tender meat and chewy gnocchi drift in a light aromatic sauce, topped by melting cheese.

FOR THE MARINATED VEAL:

1/3 cup extra-virgin olive oil

1 1/2 cups red wine

3 fresh sage leaves

1 fresh rosemary sprig

1 fresh thyme sprig

3 cloves garlic, crushed with the broad end of a
    knife blade and peeled

3 pounds veal shoulder, chuck, or neck,
    cut into 1-inch cubes

In a large nonreactive bowl, combine the olive oil, wine, sage, rosemary, thyme, and garlic. Add the veal and mix well with the marinade. Cover and refrigerate for 4 to 8 hours, or overnight.

1 large onion, minced
1 stalk celery, thinly sliced
1 small carrot, thinly sliced
6 cups chicken stock or canned low-sodium
    chicken broth
2 tablespoons tomato paste

1/2 to 1/3 pound eggplant, peeled and cut into
    1-inch cubes (about 3 1/4 cups)
1 zucchini, cut into 1/2-inch slices
Kosher salt
Freshly ground black pepper

In a medium stockpot over medium heat, combine the veal, marinade, onion, celery, carrot, stock, and tomato paste and simmer gently, stirring occasionally, for 15 minutes. Reduce the heat to medium-low, add the eggplant and zucchini, and season with salt and pepper. Continue cooking until the meat is tender, about 1 1/2 hours. Reserve. Can be refrigerated for up to 3 days.

1 1/2 pounds russet potatoes, unpeeled
Kosher salt

1 3/4 cups unbleached all-purpose flour
Pinch of freshly grated nutmeg

1. Put the potatoes in a medium pot and cover with cold water. Add 1 tablespoon salt and bring to a simmer over medium-high heat. Simmer until tender, 40 to 50 minutes, depending upon the size of the potatoes.

2. Spread the flour on a work surface. While the potatoes are still hot, peel them and pass them through a food mill or ricer onto the flour. Sprinkle the potatoes with nutmeg and salt. Let them cool to room temperature.

3. Combine the potatoes with the flour, using your fingers and a dough scraper, and gather the dough into a ball. Cut the dough into 8 pieces. Roll each piece into a thin log

(about the width of your finger), and cut into 1/2-inch pieces with a sharp knife. Roll each of the gnocchi over a fork or a grater to obtain grooves. (The gnocchi can be refrigerated for up to 2 days. Toss with a little flour or cornmeal so the pieces don't stick to one another. Bring to room temperature before cooking.)

4. Bring a large pot of water to a boil and add the gnocchi. Let them cook for 3 to 4 minutes; they will rise to the surface when done. Remove with a slotted spoon and add to the veal stew. (The gnocchi can be refrigerated for up to 2 hours or frozen for up to 1 month.)

TO COMPLETE THE STEW:

1 cup freshly grated Pecorino Romano or
    Parmigiano-Reggiano cheese

1. Preheat the oven to 350°F.

2. Spoon the stew into a medium ovenproof casserole, preferably terra-cotta, and top with the grated Pecorino Romano. Bake for about 15 minutes, or until the cheese is melted and the stew is heated through. Serve from the casserole.

Slow-Braised Veal and Vanilla Sweet Potato Shepherd's Pie

Makes 4 servings as a side dish

Expect the unexpected from Chef Hayden, of Manhattan's Amuse Restaurant. In this tantalizing combination of opposites, the sweetness of the potatoes and the earthiness of the mushrooms play counterpoint to savory veal. This fusion of sweet potatoes, leeks, and mushrooms makes a rich accompaniment to your favorite grilled veal chops.

FOR THE BRAISED VEAL:

8 ounces boneless veal breast
Kosher salt
Freshly ground black pepper
2 tablespoons canola oil

8 ounces demi-glace (see Sources; or substitute
    veal or chicken stock or canned
    low-sodium chicken broth)

1. Preheat the oven to 325°F.

2. Season the veal breast with salt and pepper. In an ovenproof sauté pan large enough to accommodate the meat, heat the canola oil over medium-high heat until very hot, and sear the veal breast on both sides. Drain the excess oil, add the demi-glace, and bring to a boil.

3. Cover the pan with foil and place it in the oven. Braise for 1 hour, or until the meat starts to separate when pulled at with a fork.

4. Pour the contents of the pan into a colander set over a large bowl and separate the meat and the juices. Cut the meat into 1/4-inch dice and reserve both the meat and the juices.

1 1/2 pounds sweet potatoes, peeled
1/2 vanilla bean
6 tablespoons unsalted butter, at
    room temperature
1 tablespoon maple syrup
Kosher salt

Freshly ground black pepper
2 large leeks (white and 1/2 inch of green),
    washed and cut into 1/2-inch dice
8 shiitake mushroom caps, cut into
    1/2-inch dice
1 tablespoon chopped fresh chives

1. Cut up enough sweet potatoes to make 1 cup of 1/2-inch dice, and reserve the rest for the purée. Put the sweet potato dice in a medium pot of cold salted water and bring to a boil. Cook for 1 minute and drain. Let the potatoes cool; they should have a slight bite. Reserve.

2. Put the remaining sweet potatoes in another pot of cold salted water and bring to a boil. Cook until very tender (20 to 30 minutes), and drain. Keep the potatoes in the covered pot, off the heat, for 2 minutes, to steam. Transfer the steamed potatoes to a food processor. Scrape in the vanilla bean seeds, and add 2 tablespoons of the butter, the maple syrup, and salt and pepper to taste. Process to a very smooth purée. Let cool and reserve.

3. In a sauté pan over medium heat, melt 2 tablespoons of the butter. Add the diced leek and cook for 2 minutes. Add the diced shiitake and cook for 2 minutes more, or until the vegetables are soft. Season to taste with salt and pepper. Let cool and reserve.

4. In a mixing bowl, combine the reserved diced veal, the sweet potato dice, the leek-and-shiitake mixture, the chives, and the remaining 2 tablespoons butter. Add the reserved veal juices, season to taste with and salt and pepper, and mix well.

1. Preheat the oven to 375°F.

2. Spread the veal mixture evenly over the bottom of a medium casserole dish, then spread the sweet potato purée evenly over the top of the veal. Cover with foil and bake for 20 minutes, or until the mixture is heated through (when the tip of a knife inserted and removed is hot to the touch). Remove the foil and bake for 10 minutes more, or until the top is slightly golden. Serve from the baking dish.

VEAL

Veal Croquettes with Dilled New Potatoes

Makes 4 servings

Golden, delicate cakes of ground veal need a gentle accompaniment, and they find their ideal match in new potatoes perfumed with sprigs of fresh dill. The light flavors of the veal and the potatoes delicately complement one another, and your favorite bright green vegetable will complete the plate.

FOR THE VEAL CROQUETTES:

12 ounces ground veal
3/4 cup plain bread crumbs
1/2 teaspoon kosher salt
1/4 teaspoon freshly ground black pepper

1/4 teaspoon ground nutmeg
1/2 cup half-and-half
2 tablespoons canola oil

1. In a mixing bowl, combine the veal, 1/2 cup of the bread crumbs, the salt, pepper, and nutmeg. Mix in the half-and-half with a wooden spoon until completely absorbed.

2. Divide the veal mixture into 4 portions and form each into an even patty, about 1/2 inch thick. Put the patties on a plate and sprinkle on both sides with the remaining 1/4 cup bread crumbs, pressing the crumbs into the meat.

3. In a medium skillet, preferably nonstick, heat the canola oil over medium-high heat. Cook the veal croquettes until golden, about 3 minutes on each side; reduce the heat to medium-low and cover the pan. Continue cooking until the croquettes are cooked through, 5 to 7 minutes more.

2 pounds new potatoes, unpeeled
Kosher salt
3 tablespoons unsalted butter, at room tem-
perature, cut into small chunks

1/2 cup minced fresh dill, plus fresh dill sprigs
Freshly ground black pepper

1. Put the potatoes in a medium pot and cover with cold water. Add 1 tablespoon salt and bring to a simmer over medium-high heat. Simmer until the potatoes are tender, 25 to 30 minutes.

2. Drain the potatoes in a colander and immediately return them to the pot. With a wooden spoon, mix in the butter and minced dill. Smash the potatoes slightly with the spoon, and season with salt and pepper.

SERVE   the potatoes alongside the croquettes, and garnish with fresh dill sprigs.

Baeckoefe (Alsatian Meat-and-Potato Casserole)

Makes 6 servings

Chef Bertineau, of Manhattan's Payard Pâtisserie and Bistro, tells us that in the Alsatian countryside, farmers traditionally brought casseroles of mixed meats and potatoes to the village baker to cook while they were working in the fields. Although the casseroles baked most of the day until the farmers' return, in your home oven, the dish can be done in considerably less time.

Lard is traditional for greasing the terrine, but you can also use butter or duck fat.

FOR THE MARINATED BEEF, LAMB, AND PORK:

1 (750-milliliter) bottle Alsatian Pinot Blanc wine, or substitute Riesling
2 onions, cut into small dice
2 whole cloves
1 fresh thyme sprig
8 cloves garlic, crushed with the broad end of a knife blade and peeled
Kosher salt

Freshly ground black pepper
1 pound beef top round, cut into 1¹/₂-inch chunks
1 pound boneless lamb leg or shoulder, cut into 1¹/₂-inch chunks
1 pound pork shoulder or butt, cut into 1¹/₂-inch chunks

In a large nonreactive bowl, combine the wine, onions, cloves, thyme, garlic, and salt and pepper to taste. Add the beef, lamb, and pork, and stir to cover well with the marinade. Cover and refrigerate for at least 8 hours or overnight.

1 to 2 tablespoons unsalted butter, plus extra
      for greasing the terrine (or substitute
      lard or duck fat, see Sources)
2 1/2 pounds Yukon Gold potatoes, unpeeled
1 large onion, thinly sliced

Kosher salt
Freshly ground black pepper
1 1/3 cups beef stock or canned low-sodium
      beef broth

1. Drain the meat in a colander set over a bowl. Reserve the marinade and the meat, and discard the other solids.

2. Preheat the oven to 325°F. Lightly butter a 13 by 9-inch casserole or a round 3- to 4-quart casserole.

3. Peel and slice the potatoes 1/4 inch thick and immediately begin to layer them in the casserole. Do not put the potatoes in water; it is important that they retain their starch.

4. Starting and ending with the potatoes, make layers of potatoes, onion, and meat, seasoning each layer with salt and pepper. The final layer of potatoes can be formed into a decorative pattern by making a rectangle or circle of potatoes just within the outer rim of the casserole and then forming increasingly smaller inner rectangles or circles until you reach the middle. Decorate the top with any leftover slices.

5. Combine 1 1/3 cups of the reserved marinade with the stock, and pour the liquid into and around the layers, coming just to the top of the potatoes but not covering them. Dot the top with the butter.

6. Cover tightly with a lid and place in the oven for 2 hours. Remove the lid and bake for 1 hour more, to reduce the juices and caramelize the top. If the meat and potatoes are not yet tender, continue baking until the desired doneness is reached.

SERVE   from the casserole with a green salad and the same Pinot Blanc or Riesling used in the marinade.

La Svizzera (Italian-Style Hamburgers) with Prosciutto Mashed Potatoes

Makes 4 servings

Chef Pellegrino, of Manhattan's Baldoria Restaurant, tells us that in northern Italy, hamburgers are called *Svizzera* because the Swiss were the first Europeans to fall in love with the American creation. Whatever the name, this is a fabulous Italian dish!

A few tips: This recipe will make 4 generous burgers; you can make 6 smaller portions, if you prefer. It's a good idea to start the potatoes first and prepare the burgers while they are cooking. And for a great meatball recipe, simply add an egg to the meat mixture—but if you do, be sure to cook the meatballs at a lower temperature.

FOR THE PROSCIUTTO MASHED POTATOES:

*2 pounds russet potatoes, peeled and
quartered
Kosher salt
1 cup whole milk
1/4 cup corn oil
1 large onion, thinly sliced*

*1/2 pound (2 sticks) plus 2 tablespoons
unsalted butter, the 1/2 pound diced
Freshly ground white pepper
Pinch of ground nutmeg
8 ounces prosciutto, cut into 1/2-inch dice*

1. Put the potatoes in a large pot and cover with cold water. Add 1 tablespoon salt and bring to a low boil over medium-high heat. Cook until tender when pierced with the tip of a knife, about 25 minutes.

2. While the potatoes are cooking, bring the milk to a boil in a small pot over medium heat.

3. Place a medium sauté pan over medium heat for 3 minutes. Add the corn oil and heat until smoking. Reduce the heat to medium-low, add the sliced onion, and cook, stirring occasionally, until translucent, about 15 minutes. Add the 2 tablespoons butter and cook, stirring often, until the onion turns a caramel color, another 12 to 15 minutes.

4. Drain the potatoes and pass through a food mill or ricer back into their cooking pot, off the heat. Add half of the diced butter and mix well until the butter is fully incorporated. Gradually mix in the remaining diced butter. Add 3/4 cup of the hot milk, mix well, and add the remaining 1/4 cup, as needed. Season with white pepper, the nutmeg, and additional salt, if needed.

5. Place the pot over low heat and stir in the caramelized onion and the prosciutto. Cook, stirring often, for 3 minutes.

FOR THE HAMBURGERS:

1 pound ground beef chuck
8 ounces ground veal
8 ounces ground pork
1/2 teaspoon minced garlic
2 tablespoons freshly grated Parmesan cheese
2 tablespoons finely chopped shallots
    or white onion
1/4 cup corn oil

Kosher salt
Freshly ground black pepper
4 good-quality hamburger buns, halved
4 slices Swiss, Cheddar, or American cheese
    (optional)
Mayonnaise (optional)
4 slices beefsteak tomato
4 Boston lettuce leaves, washed and patted dry

1. Preheat the oven to 400°F.

2. In a large nonreactive bowl, using your hands, combine the beef, veal, and pork. Add the garlic, Parmesan cheese, shallots, and 2 tablespoons of the corn oil, and mix well. Season with salt and pepper.

3. Divide the meat mixture into 4 patties, about 1 inch thick, and flatten the surfaces.

4. Heat a large ovenproof sauté pan over medium heat for 3 minutes; add the remaining 2 tablespoons corn oil and heat for 2 to 3 minutes more. Add the hamburgers and sear until brown, 4 to 5 minutes on each side.

5. Put the pan in the oven and cook to the desired doneness (3 to 4 minutes for medium-rare, 12 minutes for medium-well). Put the buns in the oven for about 3 minutes, to toast.

6. If you want to make cheeseburgers, top each patty with a slice of the cheese for the last 2 minutes of cooking.

7. Spread 4 of the bun halves with the mayonnaise, if using, and place a burger, a slice of tomato, and a lettuce leaf on each. Top with the other half of the bun.

S E R V E   the *Svizzera* alongside a mound of the prosciutto mashed potatoes.

4.

Lamb, Venison, and Potatoes

*P*OTATOES HAVE ALWAYS BEEN NATURAL PARTNERS FOR the assertive flavor of lamb, and these recipes include Red Bliss, creamer, russet, Yukon Gold, red new, purple, and fingerling. Sometimes the potatoes provide a quiet balance to the meat, and sometimes they do the unexpected and yell even louder.

In John Sundstrom's Herb-Grilled Lamb Chops with Chanterelle and Potato Hash, golden, red, and purple potatoes more than hold their own beside herb-accented grilled loin chops. In Jean-Louis Gerin's Lamb Chops Champvallon, both the chops—this time from the shoulder—and the potatoes are treated gently, simply layered with onions and baked until succulent. In Thomas John's Indian-Spiced Rack of Lamb with Potato Tikki and Mint Yogurt, the lamb is cut into separate chops after the rack has been roasted; it is served with cumin-and-coriander-spiced potato cakes and a cooling minted yogurt sauce.

Lamb shanks require a longer cooking time than chops or a rack of lamb, but for Daniel Angerer's Potato-Crusted Lamb Cakes, the meat can be slowly braised and then crusted with thinly sliced potatoes ahead of time, and reheated quickly when you are ready to serve.

Roast leg of lamb with potatoes is a perfect party dish, and you can give it either a French or a Greek accent. Sandro Gamba flavors his roast with curry and lemon and accompanies it with his grandmother Jeannette's beyond-heavenly truffled mashed potatoes. Cooking in a different style, Jim Botsacos flavors leg of lamb with lusty garlic, Greek oregano, and olive oil, and roasts it along with onions and potatoes. He completes the picture with a spicy, colorful okra, onion, and tomato stew.

Mark Franz's Slow-Roasted Lamb Shoulder with Potatoes, Garlic, and Rosemary is a boneless rolled roast that is herbaceous and delicious, and its potatoes absorb aromatic juices as the dish slowly cooks.

I had been searching for an old-fashioned Irish stew, but Frank Coe offered a much more exciting dish ("I haven't made Irish stew for years," he informed me). His lamb and potatoes are flavored with a variety of herbs and spices, along with dried figs and apricots and pomegranate molasses. I turned to my kitchen for a shepherd's pie that is a lot like the favorite you remember from your own childhood, with savory ground lamb under a topping of golden-crusted mashed potatoes. And for a touch of Middle Eastern style, try Lamb-Stuffed Potato Kubbeh, crusty mashed-potato cakes filled with a mixture of sautéed ground lamb and sweet raisins.

In an elegant dish from their Maine restaurant, Mark Gaier and Clark Frasier pair lean, marinated venison with rich sweet potatoes. Arrows' Leg of Venison with Roasted Yams is not an everyday meat-and-potatoes combination, but it is a perfect one.

LAMB

Herb-Grilled Lamb Chops with Chanterelle and Potato Hash

Makes 6 servings

Forget hash browns! This is the most beautiful potato hash ever, resplendent with gold, purple, and white potatoes and golden mushrooms, from Chef Sundstrom of Seattle's Earth and Ocean. Juicy grilled lamb chops that have been bathed in an herbal marinade complete the striking dish.

FOR THE MARINATED LAMB CHOPS:

1/4 cup extra-virgin olive oil

6 fresh summer savory sprigs, leaves stripped
    and chopped

6 fresh rosemary sprigs, leaves stripped and
    chopped

6 fresh thyme sprigs, leaves stripped and
    chopped

4 cloves garlic, minced

Kosher or coarse salt

Freshly ground black pepper

12 double-cut lamb loin chops, Frenched

In a large bowl, combine the olive oil, savory, rosemary, thyme, garlic, salt, and pepper. Add the lamb chops and toss to coat them well with the marinade. Cover and refrigerate for at least 4 hours or up to 24 hours.

4 tablespoons unsalted butter

1 pound Yukon Gold potatoes, unpeeled, cut into 3/8-inch dice

Kosher salt

Freshly ground black pepper

1 pound red new potatoes, unpeeled, cut into 3/8-inch dice

1 pound purple potatoes, unpeeled, cut into 3/8-inch dice

1 pound golden chanterelle mushrooms, quartered

2 yellow onions, cut into 1/4-inch dice

4 cloves garlic, minced

1 bunch of scallions (white and 3 inches of green), thinly sliced

1. Heat a large nonstick pan over medium heat. Melt 1 tablespoon of the butter and cook the Yukon Gold potatoes, allowing them to brown slightly on all sides and to become crisp yet tender. Toss often and season lightly with salt and pepper. Remove to a plate.

2. Repeat with 1 tablespoon of butter and the red new potatoes.

3. Repeat with 1 tablespoon of butter and the purple potatoes.

4. Add the remaining 1 tablespoon butter and cook the chanterelles and onions until the mushrooms are tender and the onions are softened, about 8 minutes. Add the garlic and cook until softened, about 2 minutes. Leave the mushroom mixture in the pan. Return all the potatoes to the pan and combine well. Add the scallions and cook for 1 minute. Season again with salt and pepper, and reserve.

TO GRILL THE LAMB CHOPS:

Canola oil
Kosher salt
Freshly ground black pepper

1. Preheat a charcoal or gas grill and brush the rack with an oiled paper towel. (Or preheat a heavy stovetop grill pan or the broiler.)
2. Remove the lamb chops from the marinade and let them come to room temperature. Season them with salt and pepper, and grill to the desired doneness (8 to 10 minutes for medium-rare). Let the chops rest in a warm place for 5 to 6 minutes before serving.

TO SERVE:

Chopped flat-leaf parsley

Divide the chanterelle and potato hash evenly among 6 serving plates and top with the lamb chops. Garnish with chopped parsley.

LAMB

JEAN-LOUIS GERIN

Lamb Chops Champvallon

Makes 4 servings

A simple, earthy pairing of tender lamb chops and sliced potatoes, this classic French dish, from the chef and owner of Restaurant Jean-Louis, in Greenwich, Connecticut, is said to have first been introduced in the court of Louis XIV. Champvallon is for true potato lovers—there will be generous leftovers to enjoy.

4 shoulder lamb chops, about 1/2 inch thick
Kosher salt
Freshly ground black pepper
2 tablespoons unsalted butter
6 cups unsalted chicken stock or canned
    low-sodium chicken broth
1 bay leaf

1 fresh thyme sprig
4 to 5 russet potatoes, peeled and sliced
    1/4 inch thick (6 cups)
3 to 4 onions, sliced 1/4 inch thick (2 cups)
2 tablespoons minced scallions (white and
    2 inches of green)

1. Preheat the oven to 350°F.
2. Season the lamb chops with salt and pepper.
3. In a large skillet over medium-high heat, melt the butter and sauté the chops until lightly browned, about 2 minutes on each side. Add the chicken stock, bay leaf, and thyme, and bring to a boil. Remove from the heat.
4. Place half of the potato slices in a thin layer on the bottom of a gratin dish, sprinkle lightly with salt and pepper, and cover with half of the onion slices. Arrange the lamb

chops over the onions. Top with the remaining onion slices, and finish with a layer of the remaining potato slices. Season with salt and pepper.

5. Pour the chicken stock mixture over the dish and cover tightly with foil. Bake for 40 minutes, then remove the foil and continue baking for 15 to 30 minutes more, until the potatoes and meat are tender and the potatoes are golden. Remove the bay leaf and thyme sprig, sprinkle with the scallions, and serve immediately on warmed plates.

Indian-Spiced Rack of Lamb with Potato Tikki and Mint Yogurt

Makes 2 servings

Herbs and freshly toasted spices—cilantro leaves, fresh mint, cumin and coriander seeds—are Chef John's gift to meat and potatoes. In his Mantra Restaurant, in Boston, tender rack of lamb is paired with crisp, spicy Indian potato cakes, and the combination is served with a cooling minted yogurt sauce.

FOR THE MINT YOGURT:

1/2 cup fresh mint leaves
1/2 cup fresh cilantro leaves
1 clove garlic, peeled
2 tablespoons coarsely chopped white onion

1 tablespoon freshly squeezed lime juice
1/4 cup plain yogurt, regular or fat-free
1/4 teaspoon kosher salt

Purée all the ingredients in a blender until smooth. The sauce can be refrigerated for up to 3 days; bring it to room temperature before serving.

1 1/2 teaspoons freshly cracked black pepper
   (see Note)
1 tablespoon cumin seeds
1/2 teaspoon kosher salt, or to taste
2 tablespoons red wine vinegar

1 tablespoon extra-virgin olive oil
1 tablespoon plain yogurt, regular or fat-free
1 rack of lamb, chine bone removed and
   trimmed of excess fat (the butcher can
   do this)

1. Combine the black pepper, cumin seeds, salt, vinegar, olive oil, and yogurt in a large bowl. Add the lamb, cover, and marinate for 30 minutes or up to 1 hour.

2. Preheat the broiler.

3. Remove the lamb from the marinade, shaking off any excess liquid. Place the lamb under the broiler, meat side up, and cook to the desired doneness (15 minutes for medium-rare). Remove the lamb from the broiler and let it rest for 5 minutes, tented with foil. Slice into chops, using a sharp knife.

1 large russet potato, unpeeled
1/2 teaspoon cumin seeds
1/2 teaspoon coriander seeds
1 clove garlic, minced

2 tablespoons minced white onion
Juice of 1/2 lemon
Kosher salt
1 tablespoon grapeseed oil

1. Preheat the oven to 350°F and bake the potato for about 45 minutes, or until tender (or microwave the potato until tender).

2. In a small dry pan, toast the cumin and coriander seeds over medium-high heat until fragrant, about 4 minutes, shaking the pan often. Grind the seeds to a powder in a spice grinder, coffee grinder, or mortar and pestle.

3. When the potato is cool enough to handle, peel and grate it finely. Place the grated potato in a mixing bowl and add the garlic, onion, ground cumin and coriander, lemon juice, and salt. Mix lightly and form the mixture into 2 square cakes, 1/2 to 1 inch thick

4. In a medium pan, heat the grapeseed oil over medium-high heat and cook the cakes until brown and crisp on both sides and warmed through, 6 to 8 minutes.

TO SERVE, place 1 sautéed potato cake in the center of each plate. Arrange the lamb chops around the potato cake, and ladle mint yogurt around the lamb.

NOTE: For cracked black pepper, wrap peppercorns in a dish towel and smash them with a heavy pan.

Potato-Crusted Lamb Cakes

Makes 4 servings

Chef Angerer, of Fresh restaurant in Tribeca, braises lamb shanks with fragrant spices and herbs, and uses the classic technique of wrapping in caul fat, in his preparation of individual crisp-crusted cakes. You can cook the lamb ahead of time and form the cakes up to 4 days before you are ready to do the final cooking. This elegant entrée will then take less than half an hour to put on the table.

FOR THE BRAISED LAMB SHANKS:

3 large lamb shanks (3 to 4 pounds total)
Kosher salt
Freshly ground black pepper
2 tablespoons canola oil
2 carrots, cut into 1-inch dice
2 onions, cut into 1-inch dice
1 celery root, cut into 1-inch dice

3 cups red wine, preferably Merlot
2 cups chicken stock or canned low-sodium
    chicken broth
2 tablespoons coriander seeds
2 tablespoons pink peppercorns
2 bay leaves
2 fresh rosemary sprigs

1. Preheat the oven to 350°F.
2. Sprinkle the lamb shanks generously with salt and pepper.
3. In a large ovenproof pot over medium-high heat, heat the canola oil and brown the meat evenly on all sides. Transfer the meat to a plate and pour off all but 1 tablespoon of the fat.
4. Add the carrots, onions, and celery root to the pot and cook until browned, about 10 minutes. Add the red wine and chicken stock. Wrap the coriander seeds, peppercorns,

bay leaves, and rosemary in a square of cheesecloth and add the sachet to the pot. Bring the liquid to a boil, add the lamb shanks, and cover.

5. Transfer the pot to the oven. Braise the lamb shanks until the meat falls off the bone, 2 to 2½ hours.

6. Drain the meat and vegetables in a colander over a large bowl, reserving the braising liquid. Discard the herbs and bones.

FOR THE POTATO-CRUSTED LAMB CAKES:

2 large russet potatoes, peeled

2 ounces caul fat (lining of a pork stomach, may be ordered from your butcher), soaked in water, patted dry, and cut into 4 equal pieces

2 tablespoons canola oil

1. Put the lamb-and-vegetable mixture into four 4-inch, 1-inch high, ring molds (see Note). Press the mixture down with a spoon. Refrigerate for about 30 minutes, or until firm.

2. Meanwhile, slice the potatoes paper thin (using a mandoline, if possible).

3. When the lamb cakes are cool, layer the potatoes onto the top of each, dividing the potatoes equally. Remove the cakes from the molds and wrap each tightly with the caul fat, as thinly as possible. The cakes may be refrigerated, well covered, for up to 4 days. In fact, they will taste even better after 1 day's refrigeration and will be more compact and easier to sear. They may be frozen, well wrapped, for up to 3 months.

4. If the oven has been turned off, preheat it again to 400°F.

5. In a large ovenproof sauté pan, heat the canola oil over medium-high heat until shimmering, and sear the lamb cakes, potato crust down, until well browned, about 5 minutes. Turn over and transfer to the oven for 10 minutes, or until heated through. If they have been refrigerated or defrosted, the cakes may take longer to reheat.

6. Serve the cakes hot from the oven.

NOTE: If you don't have ring molds, pack the meat into 1/2-pint plastic containers (the kind you get food in at the deli), or shape rings out of aluminum foil.

SANDRO GAMBA

Roasted Leg of Lamb with Grandmother Jeannette's Truffled Mashed Potatoes

Makes 6 to 8 servings

Chef Gamba, of Chicago's NoMI, pairs his grandmother's famous potato dish (from her renowned restaurant, Les Cinq Ponts, in Neufchâteau, France) with tender leg of lamb marinated in curry and lemon. The result is an elegant version of childhood memories.

FOR THE ROASTED LEG OF LAMB:

1 cup sweet curry powder
4 cups lemon olive oil (available in specialty
*   grocery stores) or extra-virgin olive oil*
1 (5- to 7-pound) leg of lamb, butterflied
Kosher salt
Freshly ground black pepper
2 tablespoons canola oil
2 carrots, cut into thick disks

2 stalks celery, cut into 1-inch pieces
2 onions, cut into 1-inch dice
1 head garlic, halved crosswise
1/4 cup black peppercorns
2 bay leaves
2 cups apple juice
2 cups chicken stock or canned low-sodium
*   chicken broth*

1. In a deep nonreactive bowl that is large enough to accommodate the lamb, combine the curry powder and the lemon olive oil.

2. Spread the lamb on a work surface and brush on the marinade. Roll the lamb into a cylinder (keep the fattier side outside) and tie it with butcher's string. Put the lamb into the marinade bowl, coat with the remaining marinade, cover, and refrigerate for 24 hours.

3. Preheat the oven to 350°F.

4. Remove the lamb from the bowl and shake off any excess marinade. Season the lamb with salt and pepper. In a large sauté pan over medium-high heat, heat the canola oil and sear the lamb until golden brown on all sides; remove it from the pan.

5. Add the carrots, celery, onions, and garlic to the pan and sauté them in the remaining oil, over medium-high heat, until lightly browned. Season the vegetables with salt and pepper.

6. Lay the vegetables, peppercorns, and bay leaves in the bottom of a roasting pan (about 12 by 9 by 4 inches) and place the lamb on top of them. Add the apple juice and chicken stock. Roast the lamb until the internal temperature reaches 140°F for medium-rare, $1^1/4$ to $1^1/2$ hours. Strain the cooking liquid and reserve. If you want a thicker sauce, reduce the liquid over high heat to the desired thickness.

FOR THE TRUFFLED MASHED POTATOES:

2 pounds Yukon Gold potatoes, peeled
Kosher salt
1 cup whole milk

2 tablespoons heavy cream
4 ounces truffle butter (see Sources)
Freshly ground black pepper

1. Put the potatoes in a medium pot and cover with lightly salted cold water. Bring to a simmer over medium-high heat and cook until fork-tender, 35 to 40 minutes. Do not allow the water to boil; lower the heat, if necessary, to keep it at a simmer. Drain the potatoes and pass them through a food mill or ricer into a mixing bowl.

2. Meanwhile, in a small pan over low heat, gently heat the milk and the heavy cream to a simmer.

3. Add the milk, cream, and truffle butter to the potatoes. Mix, using a wooden spoon, until the potatoes are smooth and creamy. Be careful not to overmix the potatoes, or they will become pasty. Season with salt and pepper

TO SERVE, allow the lamb to rest for 15 minutes, tented with foil. Remove the string and slice thickly. Accompany with the truffled mashed potatoes

LAMB

Roasted Greek Leg of Lamb with Rustic Potatoes and Okra, Onion, and Tomato Stew

Makes 8 servings

This is the Greek way to roast lamb and potatoes—Chef Jim Botsacos, of Manhattan's Molyvos, reinterprets a classic, beautiful dish. The colorful okra and tomato stew heightens the mellow flavors and velvety texture of the meat and potatoes.

Make the okra stew while the lamb is roasting. You will need to stir in 1 cup of the lamb cooking juices, and you can take this amount out of the roasting pan shortly before the lamb is done—the juices won't be needed until the last 15 minutes of cooking the okra.

FOR THE ROASTED LEG OF LAMB:

1 (6- to 7-pound) leg of lamb (weight with
    bone in), boned, rolled, and tied
1 clove garlic, quartered
1/4 cup plus 1 tablespoon extra-virgin olive oil
Kosher salt
Freshly ground black pepper
1 tablespoon dried Greek oregano, plus
    1 teaspoon crumbled (or substitute
    Turkish or Mediterranean, see Sources)

4 yellow onions, thinly sliced
16 small, thin-skinned potatoes (such as
    Red Bliss or creamer), unpeeled,
    quartered
Juice of 1 lemon
1/2 cup white wine
2 cups chicken stock or canned low-sodium
    chicken broth, plus more as needed

1. Make 4 random slits in the lamb and insert the garlic quarters. Rub the lamb with 1 tablespoon olive oil, and sprinkle with salt, pepper, and the 1 teaspoon crumbled oregano. Place in a nonreactive dish, cover, and refrigerate for at least 3 hours or up to 8 hours.

2. Preheat the oven to 450°F.

3. Put the lamb in a roasting pan or a casserole large enough to accommodate it (as well as the onions and potatoes that you will add later), and roast, uncovered, for 25 minutes.

4. Meanwhile, in a large nonreactive bowl, combine the onions, the potatoes, 1 tablespoon dried oregano, 1/4 cup olive oil, and the lemon juice. Season with salt and pepper, and toss lightly to combine.

5. Remove the roasting pan from the oven and reduce the oven temperature to 400°F. Pour the wine into the pan and add the onion and potato mixture, taking care to distribute it evenly around the lamb. Add the chicken stock.

6. Return the lamb to the oven and roast, uncovered, basting frequently, for another 2 hours, or until an instant-read meat thermometer reaches 140°F (this will be medium-rare). Add additional stock or water to the pan during roasting if needed. There should be at least 2 cups of lamb juices; remove 1 cup of juice about 30 minutes before the lamb is done, and use it for the okra, onion, and tomato stew, below.

7. Remove the lamb from the oven and let it rest, tented with foil, for 10 minutes before slicing.

1/4 cup plus 2 tablespoons olive oil
1 pound okra, washed and trimmed
Kosher salt
Freshly ground black pepper
4 onions, julienned
3 cloves garlic, thinly sliced
1/2 teaspoon dried Greek oregano
    (or substitute Turkish or
    Mediterranean, see Sources)

1/4 teaspoon Aleppo pepper (see Sources)
2 cups canned crushed whole tomatoes, with
    their juice (from a 28-ounce can; there
    will be some left over)
1 cup reserved lamb juices, strained
2 tablespoons sliced pitted kalamata olives
2 tablespoons chopped fresh parsley
2 tablespoons extra-virgin olive oil

1. In a large saucepan, heat 1 tablespoon of the olive oil over medium-high heat, add half the okra, and sauté until lightly seared, 2 to 3 minutes. Season with salt and black pepper. Transfer to a bowl and reserve. Reheat the pan, add another tablespoon of the olive oil, and repeat with the remaining okra.

2. In a large, heavy pot, heat the 1/4 cup olive oil over medium-high heat and add the onions. Season with a pinch of salt, stir, and cook until soft and translucent, 10 to 15 minutes. Stir in the garlic, reduce the heat to medium, and cook, stirring occasionally, until the onions are lightly caramelized, about 8 minutes more. Add the oregano and Aleppo pepper, stir, and cook for 1 minute.

3. Reduce the heat to low, stir in the tomatoes, and cook for 5 to 6 minutes. Add the reserved okra and stir to combine the ingredients. Add the lamb juices and simmer (still over low heat) for 15 to 20 minutes. When the okra is slightly tender, fold in the olives, parsley, and extra-virgin olive oil. Season with salt and black pepper.

TO SERVE, place the lamb on a large platter and remove the string. Slice the lamb to the desired thickness, and arrange the potatoes and onions around it. Serve with the okra, onion, and tomato stew.

LAMB

Slow-Roasted Lamb Shoulder with Potatoes, Garlic, and Rosemary

Makes 6 to 8 servings

Chef Franz, of San Francisco's Farallon Restaurant, makes this garlicky, herbaceous lamb in his kitchen at home. Slow roasting ensures that the lamb is tender and delicious and that the potatoes are infused with aromatic, flavorful juices.

20 cloves garlic, peeled
Kosher salt
1 (6-pound) boneless lamb shoulder,
    rolled and tied

1/2 cup chopped fresh rosemary
1/2 cup olive oil
Freshly ground black pepper
6 large russet potatoes, peeled

1. Preheat the oven to 300°F.

2. Using a mortar and pestle, crush 6 of the garlic cloves and mash into a paste with some of the kosher salt. Rub the paste into the lamb. Sprinkle the lamb all over with 1/4 cup of the rosemary and then rub with some of the olive oil. Season with more salt and the black pepper.

3. Quarter the potatoes and toss them in a bowl with the rest of the olive oil.

4. Put the lamb in a large roasting pan and tuck the potatoes and the remaining 14 garlic cloves all around (but not under) the lamb. Sprinkle with the remaining 1/4 cup rosemary. Seal the pan tightly with a double layer of foil and put it in the oven. Roast the lamb for 2 hours and then remove the foil. Increase the heat to 350°F and continue to roast the lamb for another 30 minutes.

5. Remove the lamb from the oven and allow it to rest loosely covered with the foil for 20 minutes.

6. Place the lamb on a platter and remove the string. Carve the lamb into thick slices and arrange the potatoes and garlic alongside. Pour the accumulated juices over the meat and potatoes.

FRANK COE

Chef Frank's Flavorful Lamb Stew

Makes 4 servings

This isn't your mom's Irish stew! Chef Coe, of Long Island's Wild Goose Restaurant, calls his herbaceous, fruit-accented blending of lamb and potatoes sweet, sassy, and seductive. It looks and smells irresistible, and provides a satisfying balance of flavors.

Pinch of cumin seeds
1/4 cup extra-virgin olive oil
1 1/2 pounds boneless lamb shoulder, cut into
    2-inch cubes
Sea salt or kosher salt
Freshly ground black pepper
2 shallots, finely diced
1 stalk celery, strings removed, finely diced
1 carrot, finely diced
1 leek (white and tender green parts), washed
    and finely diced
1/2 parsnip or celery root, peeled and
    finely diced
4 cloves garlic, finely diced
1 tablespoon grated orange zest (an organic
    orange is best)

3 tablespoons pomegranate molasses
    (see Sources)
4 dried figs, coarsely chopped
2 dried apricots, coarsely chopped
2 pitted prunes, coarsely chopped
12 fingerling potatoes, peeled
1 tablespoon chopped fresh thyme
1 tablespoon chopped fresh tarragon
1 tablespoon chopped fresh rosemary
1/4 teaspoon saffron threads
2 cups demi-glace (see Sources); or
    substitute veal or chicken stock.
    (Do not use canned chicken broth.)
1/2 cup tomato concassée (see Note)
1 tablespoon chopped fresh marjoram
1 tablespoon chopped fresh mint

1. In a small dry pan over medium heat, toast the cumin seeds for about 3 minutes, shaking the pan so the seeds do not burn. Reserve.

2. Preheat the oven to 300°F.

3. In a large ovenproof skillet or Dutch oven, heat 2 tablespoons of the olive oil over medium-high heat. Sprinkle the lamb cubes with salt and pepper, and sear until golden brown on all sides, about 5 minutes. Reduce the heat to low.

4. In another large skillet, heat the remaining 2 tablespoons olive oil over medium heat. Add the shallots, celery, carrot, leek, and parsnip, and cook until the vegetables are softened but not colored, 6 to 8 minutes. Add the garlic and cook until softened, 1 or 2 minutes more.

5. Add the vegetables to the lamb. Add the orange zest, reserved cumin seeds, and pomegranate molasses, and combine well. Add the figs, apricots, prunes, potatoes, thyme, tarragon, rosemary, and saffron. Add the demi-glace and tomato concassée, stir to combine, and season with salt and pepper.

6. Raise the heat to medium, bring the stew to a simmer, and place in the oven. Cook until the meat and potatoes are tender, about 1 1/2 hours.

7. Spoon into a serving bowl and sprinkle with the chopped marjoram and mint.

NOTE: To make 1/2 cup tomato concassée, bring a small pot of lightly salted water to a boil and immerse 1 ripe tomato, about 1/3 pound, cored, with a small X cut on the bottom, for 10 to 15 seconds. Remove from the water and peel—the skin should slip off easily. Halve the tomato and squeeze gently to remove the seeds and juice. Cut the flesh into 1/4-inch dice.

JOAN SCHWARTZ

LAMB

Old-Fashioned Shepherd's Pie

Makes 4 to 6 servings

In compiling the recipes for this book, I've learned a lot about shepherd's pies! This version is the mother of them all—simple, rustic, delicious, and a real lifesaver for the busy cook.

FOR THE MASHED-POTATO TOPPING:

1 1/2 pounds Yukon Gold or russet potatoes, unpeeled
Kosher salt
1/2 cup milk

2 tablespoons unsalted butter, at room temperature
1/4 teaspoon freshly ground black pepper

1. Put the potatoes in a medium pot and cover with cold water. Add 1 tablespoon salt and bring to a simmer over medium-high heat. Simmer until tender, 25 to 30 minutes. Drain the potatoes, and peel as soon as they are cool enough to handle.

2. Meanwhile, in a small pot over medium heat, or in the microwave, warm the milk.

3. Pass the potatoes through a food mill or ricer into a mixing bowl, or mash with a potato masher. Add the butter and milk, mix well with a wooden spoon, and season with 1/2 teaspoon salt and the pepper, or to taste.

2 tablespoons olive oil

1 onion, finely chopped

1 carrot, finely chopped

1 stalk celery, finely chopped

1 pound ground lamb

2 tablespoons chopped fresh rosemary

1 teaspoon kosher salt, or to taste

1/2 teaspoon freshly ground black pepper,
   or to taste

2 tablespoons plain bread crumbs or
   matzo meal

1 large egg, lightly beaten

1 cup frozen tiny peas (they do not have to
   be thawed)

1 tablespoon unsalted butter, cut into
   small chunks

1. Preheat the oven to 400°F.

2. In a medium skillet over medium heat, heat the olive oil and cook the onion, carrot, and celery until softened, about 10 minutes. Add the lamb and press down with a fork to break up any lumps. Cook, stirring, until the meat is browned, about 15 minutes. Add the rosemary, salt, and pepper, and remove the mixture to a mixing bowl.

3. Add the bread crumbs to the meat mixture and mix well. Add the egg and combine well.

4. Pour the mixture into an ungreased 8- or 9-inch square ovenproof pan. Spoon the peas evenly over the meat. Spoon the mashed potatoes over the top, leaving a rough surface, and dot with the butter. Place in the oven for 30 to 35 minutes, until heated through and slightly browned on top. Serve from the pan.

JOAN SCHWARTZ

Lamb-Stuffed Potato Kubbeh

Makes 6 servings

These crusty, savory cakes of mashed potatoes stuffed with lamb and sweet raisins are a delicious staple in Middle Eastern Jewish households. This version is adapted from the tempting *kubbeh* served at the New York home of Rachel Meer, and from the recipe created by her mother, Touba Anwarzadeh.

While the flavors are delicate, the potato cakes are hearty, and need only a simple salad as an accompaniment. Or serve single cakes as appetizers.

FOR THE LAMB STUFFING:

1/2 cup dark raisins
2 tablespoons olive oil
1 small onion, finely chopped
8 ounces ground lamb

Kosher salt
Freshly ground black pepper
2 tablespoons minced fresh parsley

1. Put the raisins in a cup and cover with warm water. Set aside until plump, about 5 minutes, and then drain.

2. In a large skillet over medium-high heat, heat the olive oil and cook the onion until golden and softened, about 5 minutes. Add the lamb, season with salt and pepper, and sauté until the meat is browned, 5 to 10 minutes, breaking it up as it cooks. Add the raisins and parsley, and set aside to cool.

2 pounds russet potatoes, unpeeled
Kosher salt
$1/4$ teaspoon freshly ground black pepper

$1/4$ cup all-purpose flour
Vegetable oil

1. Put the potatoes in a medium pot and cover with cold water. Add 1 tablespoon salt and bring to a simmer over medium-high heat. Simmer until tender, 25 to 30 minutes. Drain the potatoes, and peel as soon as they are cool enough to handle.

2. Pass the potatoes through a food mill or ricer into a mixing bowl, or mash with a potato masher. Season with $1/2$ teaspoon salt and the pepper, add the flour, and mix well. Divide into 12 balls.

3. To form the *kubbeh,* flatten 1 ball of mashed potatoes into a disk between your hands. Put about 1 tablespoon of the lamb mixture in the center, and fold the potato over to enclose the meat. Press the edges together to seal, and with both hands, shape the potato cake into a ball. Flatten into a pancake. Repeat until all the stuffed potato cakes have been formed.

4. Wipe out the large skillet used to cook the lamb and place it over medium-high heat. Pour in the vegetable oil to a depth of $1/2$ inch and heat the oil over medium-high heat to 375°F, or until a bit of potato sizzles when immersed. Place the potato cakes in the hot oil, and fry them until deep brown, 1 to 3 minutes on each side, taking care that they do not burn.

5. Remove the *kubbeh* from the oil with a slotted spoon and drain them on paper towels. Serve hot. The *kubbeh* can be refrigerated for up to 1 day or frozen. Reheat them in a little vegetable oil over medium heat.

Arrows' Leg of Venison with Roasted Yams

Makes 6 servings

This is a simple dish, as served at Arrows, the Ogunquit, Maine, rural restaurant owned by Chefs Gaier and Frasier, but the combination of marinated, roasted venison and herb-roasted sweet potatoes is inspired. Venison is a very lean meat, so be sure not to overcook it.

FOR THE ROASTED LEG OF VENISON:

2 cups red wine
2 tablespoons red wine vinegar
1 carrot, finely diced
2 stalks celery, finely diced
1 Spanish onion, finely diced
3 cloves garlic, finely sliced
2 tablespoons coarsely chopped fresh rosemary

1 tablespoon black peppercorns
1 cup plus 2 tablespoons olive oil
1 (2¹/₂- to 3-pound) leg of venison, in a single piece (available by special order from many butchers, or see Sources)
Kosher salt
Freshly ground black pepper

1. Combine the red wine, red wine vinegar, carrot, celery, onion, garlic, rosemary, peppercorns, and 1 cup olive oil in a nonreactive casserole. Place the venison in the casserole, cover, and refrigerate for 2 hours or up to 8 hours.

2. When ready to cook, preheat the oven to 375°F. Remove the venison from the marinade and sprinkle with salt and pepper.

3. In a large sauté pan over high heat, heat 2 tablespoons olive oil until very hot but not smoking, and add the venison. Reduce the heat to medium and sauté the venison until browned on one side, then flip the meat and sauté until browned on the other

side (2 to 3 minutes on each side). Turn the meat over again, put the pan in the oven, and roast until the internal temperature of the meat is 135°F for medium-rare, about 17 minutes per pound.

FOR THE ROASTED YAMS:

3 yams (about 2 pounds), peeled and cut into 1/2-inch cubes

2 tablespoons finely chopped fresh rosemary

1/2 cup finely chopped flat-leaf parsley

3 to 4 tablespoons unsalted butter, cut into small chunks

Kosher salt

Freshly ground black pepper

1. Place the yams in a nonreactive ovenproof casserole, sprinkle with the herbs, and toss with the butter. Season with salt and pepper.
2. Roast the yams in the oven (with the venison) for about 30 minutes, or until soft.

TO SERVE, slice the venison across the grain about 1/4 inch thick and divide among 6 plates along with the yams.

5.

Pork and Potatoes

*U*ERSATILE PORK CAN BE FOUND FRESH OR CURED, AND, IN FACT, IT MOST INSPIRES OUR chefs in its incarnations as bacon, ham, and sausage. Because they are so lean, the pork chops and loins in these recipes cook quickly (although you must allow some time for marination), and the cured cuts can be prepared in a flash. In all forms, this light, succulent meat pairs perfectly with Yukon Golds, russets, sweet potatoes, and red potatoes, both mature and new.

Deborah Stanton gives pork chops a citric marinade before grilling, in her Brine-Marinated Pork Chops with Scallion-Smashed Potatoes and Grilled Granny Smith Apple Slices. Bobby Flay treats tender pork and potatoes to a riot of flavors, in his New Mexican Rubbed Pork Tenderloin with Bourbon-Ancho Sauce and Roasted Garlic–Sweet Onion Potato Gratin. And for his Sweet Potato–Stuffed Roulade of Pork, Glenn Harris rolls and stuffs a lean pork loin with mashed sweet potatoes spiked with a surprising cilantro pesto.

Ham is a team player in Debra Ponzek's recipe, adding flavor and a touch of texture. Her simple and delicious Split Pea, Ham, and Potato Soup welcomes the cooler weather.

Sausage travels to Mexico, where smoky chorizo meets potatoes and tortillas, in the imaginative Chorizo, Potato, and Goat Cheese Quesadillas from Sue Torres. Maarten Pinxteren makes kielbasa a Dutch treat with bacon, mashed potatoes, and crisp greens, in his traditional Dutch Stamppot.

Crisp bacon and buttery-soft potatoes are surely a match made in heaven, and our chefs have found ingenious ways to present it. Alexandra Guarnaschelli's Bacon Lovers' Mashed Potatoes are the purest form

of this combination and will make bacon lovers of all who taste it. William Snell's golden Tartiflette de Cocotte, topped with melting Reblochon cheese, is his tempting version of a bistro favorite. And bacon and potatoes make the perfect spring salad, as Ilene Rosen found when she scouted the Union Square Greenmarket for the freshest ingredients for her Roasted New Potatoes with Bacon, Chive Flowers, and Green Tomato Dressing.

Brine-Marinated Pork Chops with Scallion-Smashed Potatoes and Grilled Granny Smith Apple Slices

Makes 4 servings

These pork chops and potatoes will look so beautiful on your table, you will imagine that you are dining at Deborah, a favorite Greenwich Village restaurant. The chops are brined, then roasted until they are golden brown and succulent. They are accompanied by silky mashed potatoes laced with scallions and accented with sweet golden apples that can be either grilled or sautéed—a delightful combination of flavors and textures.

Even given the marinating time, preparation is efficient; the dish can be served in about an hour and a half, start to finish.

FOR THE BRINE-MARINATED PORK CHOPS:

*2 cups freshly squeezed orange juice, or
    substitute good-quality purchased*
Juice of 1 lemon
Juice of 2 limes
1/2 cup kosher salt

1/4 cup sugar
2 tablespoons chopped garlic
*4 center-cut boneless pork chops (about
    9 ounces each)*

1. In a stainless steel or other nonreactive bowl, combine the orange, lemon, and lime juice. Whisk in the salt, sugar, and garlic.

2. Pour the brine mixture into a large plastic bag, preferably Ziploc. Add the pork chops, and squeeze the air out of the bag. Seal the bag and refrigerate for 30 minutes.

FOR THE SCALLION-SMASHED POTATOES:

2 1/2 pounds Yukon Gold potatoes, unpeeled,
    cut into large dice
Kosher salt
2 cups heavy cream
4 tablespoons unsalted butter, cut into
    1/2-inch pieces

Freshly ground black pepper
2 scallions (white and 3 inches of green), finely
    chopped

1. Put the potatoes in a large pot and cover with cold water. Add 1 tablespoon salt and bring to a simmer over medium-high heat. Simmer until fork-tender, about 25 minutes.

2. While the potatoes are cooking, pour the cream into a small saucepan and bring to a scald over medium heat.

3. Drain the potatoes in a colander and put in a mixing bowl. Smash, using a potato masher or fork, blending in the butter, cream, and salt and pepper to taste. This should be a rough mixture, not a purée. Fold in the chopped scallions.

FOR THE OPTIONAL LEEK GARNISH:

About 3 1/2 cups canola oil
1 leek (white and tender green parts), cleaned
    and sliced lengthwise into fine julienne
Kosher salt

Set a sauté pan, or a heavy stovetop grill pan that you can later use for the pork chops, over medium-high heat. Heat 1/2 inch of canola oil to 350°F and fry the leek until golden brown, 8 to 10 minutes. Drain on paper towels. Sprinkle with salt, and reserve.

1. Preheat a charcoal or gas grill to moderately hot and carefully brush the rack with an oiled paper towel. Or preheat the oven to 350°F, preheat a heavy stovetop grill pan, and brush the pan with an oiled paper towel.

2. Remove the pork chops from the marinade and rinse with cold water. Pat dry. If using a grill, sear the chops on both sides, and cook to an internal temperature of 140°F. Or sear over high heat in the heated pan for 3 minutes on each side, and place in the oven until cooked to an internal temperature of 140°F (this will take about 15 minutes per inch of thickness).

3. Allow the chops to rest for 5 minutes, then slice 1/2 inch thick.

FOR THE GRILLED APPLES:

2 Granny Smith apples, sliced 1/2 inch thick (if sautéing, cut the apples into small dice)
Canola oil (if sautéing, substitute 1 tablespoon unsalted butter)

Kosher salt
Freshly ground black pepper

1. Lightly coat the apple slices with canola oil, if grilling, and season with salt and pepper. If sautéing, season the diced apples with salt and pepper.

2. Place the apple slices on the grill with the chops until golden and softened, 8 to 10 minutes. Or in a medium skillet over medium heat, melt the butter and sauté the diced apples until golden and softened, 8 to 10 minutes.

TO SERVE, divide the smashed potatoes among 4 plates, spooning them down the center. Top with the sliced pork. Fan the grilled apple slices, or arrange the sautéed diced apples, alongside the pork, and top with the fried leek, if desired.

PORK

New Mexican Rubbed Pork Tenderloin with Bourbon-Ancho Sauce and Roasted Garlic–Sweet Onion Potato Gratin

Makes 4 servings

At first reading, you might think that the bourbon-ancho sauce could be optional, since there are so many contrasting, bold notes in the New Mexican spice rub. But be sure to include this sauce! Its mellow richness works magic in bringing together all the elements of this complex dish from Bobby Flay, of Manhattan's Mesa Grill and Bolo, and television's Food Network. It is nothing short of amazing.

Bobby accompanies the deep reddish-brown crusted pork roast with a gratin of potatoes, sweet onions, and melted cotija cheese.

Both the spice rub and the sauce can be made ahead; and the gratin can be constructed a few hours ahead and refrigerated, tightly covered, until cooking time.

FOR THE NEW MEXICAN SPICE RUB:

3 tablespoons ground ancho chili pepper
   (see Sources)
2 tablespoons packed light brown sugar
1 tablespoon ground pasilla chili pepper
   (see Sources)

1 tablespoon kosher salt
2 teaspoons ground chile de arbol
   (see Sources)
2 teaspoons ground cinnamon
2 teaspoons ground allspice

Combine all the ingredients in a small bowl and reserve. This is more than you will need for the pork; store the remainder tightly covered for up to 3 months. Makes just over 1/2 cup.

2 cups heavy cream

1 head garlic, roasted, cloves peeled and puréed (see Note)

2 tablespoons olive oil

1 tablespoon unsalted butter

2 large sweet onions (such as Vidalia or Walla Walla), halved and thinly sliced

Kosher salt

Freshly ground black pepper

4 large russet or Yukon Gold potatoes, peeled and cut crosswise into 1/8-inch-thick slices

1/4 cup grated cotija cheese

1. Preheat the oven to 375°F.

2. In a medium nonreactive saucepan over medium heat, bring the cream to a simmer and whisk in the puréed roasted garlic.

3. In a large skillet over medium heat, heat the olive oil and butter and add the onions. Season with salt and pepper and cook until soft, about 20 minutes.

4. In a 9-inch square casserole, make a layer of one-eighth of the potato slices and season with salt and pepper. Top with one-eighth of the onions and drizzle with 1/4 cup of the cream. Repeat to make 8 layers.

5. Cover with foil and bake for 30 minutes. Remove the foil, sprinkle the cheese evenly over the top layer, and bake until the potatoes are tender and golden brown on top, about 20 minutes.

2 tablespoons olive oil

1 red onion, finely chopped

2 cups plus 2 tablespoons bourbon whiskey

3 ancho chiles, soaked, stemmed, seeded, and
    puréed

6 cups chicken stock or canned low-sodium
    chicken broth

1 cup frozen apple juice concentrate, thawed

8 black peppercorns

1/4 cup packed light brown sugar

Kosher salt

1. In a medium saucepan over medium-high heat, heat the olive oil and cook the onion until softened, about 10 minutes. Add 2 cups bourbon and cook until it is completely reduced and almost dry, about 10 minutes. Add the ancho chile purée, chicken stock, apple juice concentrate, peppercorns, and light brown sugar, and cook until the mixture is reduced by half, about 20 minutes.

2. Strain through a fine-mesh sieve and return the mixture to the pan. Cook over medium heat to a sauce consistency (it should coat the back of a spoon). Add 2 tablespoons bourbon and cook for 2 minutes more. Season with salt. Reserve the sauce over very low heat. May be refrigerated for up to 2 days, or frozen. Makes 1 cup.

FOR THE PORK TENDERLOIN:

1 (2-pound) pork tenderloin

Kosher salt

New Mexican Spice Rub

2 tablespoons olive oil

1. Preheat the oven to 375°F.

2. Season the pork with salt on both sides. Dredge the pork in the spice rub and tap off any excess.

3. In a medium ovenproof sauté pan or skillet over high heat, heat the olive oil until smoking, and sear the pork until golden brown on both sides. Place the pan in the oven and cook the pork to medium doneness, 8 to 10 minutes. Tent with foil and allow to rest for 5 minutes.

TO SERVE, slice the tenderloin and divide among 4 plates; spoon some sauce over the slices. Spoon some gratin alongside the pork. Pass the remaining sauce separately.

NOTE: To roast a head of garlic, rub it with olive oil and wrap it loosely in foil. Roast at 300°F for 45 minutes, or until soft.

GLENN HARRIS

Sweet Potato–Stuffed Roulade of Pork

Makes 6 to 8 servings

This moist and fragrant combination of juicy pork, aromatic pesto, and mellow sweet potatoes comes from Manhattan's Jane Restaurant, where Glenn Harris creates tantalizing new American bistro food. He suggests your favorite roasted brussels sprouts as a crisp green accompaniment.

FOR THE SWEET POTATOES:

Kosher salt
2 large sweet potatoes, peeled and julienned

Bring a medium pot of salted water to a boil over medium-high heat. Add the sweet potatoes and boil gently until tender, about 3 minutes. Drain the potatoes and place on paper towels to dry and cool.

FOR THE MARINADE:

2 tablespoons dried oregano
1 tablespoon paprika
1 tablespoon ground cumin
1 tablespoon freshly ground black pepper
1 tablespoon ground fennel seeds (see Note)

1 cup sugar
1 tablespoon kosher salt
1 tablespoon olive oil
1/2 cup water

In a small dry skillet over medium heat, combine the oregano, paprika, cumin, pepper, and ground fennel, and toast, stirring, for 3 minutes. Pour into a bowl and stir in the sugar and salt. Add the olive oil and water and mix well. Reserve.

FOR THE PESTO:

2 jalapeño peppers, stemmed and seeded
    (wash your hands well after touching
    the peppers)
4 ounces pine nuts
1 bunch of fresh cilantro, washed, heavy stems
    removed, and coarsely chopped

3 cloves garlic, coarsely chopped
Kosher salt
Freshly ground black pepper

Put the jalapeños, pine nuts, cilantro, and garlic in a food processor and blend to a paste. Season with salt and pepper. Reserve.

FOR THE PORK ROULADE:

1 (2- to 3-pound) boneless center-cut pork loin,
    butterflied (the butcher can do this)

1. In a mixing bowl, combine the sweet potatoes and the pesto. Place the butterflied pork loin on a work surface and spread the sweet potato mixture evenly over it, leaving a 1/2-inch border all around. Roll as tightly as possible, as for a jelly roll, without squeezing out any of the filling, and tie with butcher's string.

2. Place the roll in a nonreactive pan and cover with the marinade. Cover and refrigerate for at least 1 hour or up to 8 hours.

3. When ready to cook, preheat the oven to 350°F.

4. Roast the roulade, uncovered, still in the marinade, until the internal temperature reaches 140°F, about 1 hour. Remove from the oven and let rest, tented with foil, for 20 minutes.

FOR THE SAUCE:

1¹/₂ cups balsamic vinegar   3 cups apple cider

In a medium pot over medium-high heat, combine the balsamic vinegar and the apple cider and bring to a gentle boil. Cook until reduced by two-thirds, about 1 hour.

TO SERVE,   place the roulade on a platter and remove the string. Slice to the desired thickness. Spoon a little sauce over each serving.

NOTE: Fennel seeds are usually sold whole; grind them at home in a spice grinder, coffee grinder that you reserve for spices and seeds, or mortar and pestle.

Split Pea, Ham, and Potato Soup

Makes 4 to 6 servings

This simple, perfect soup from Chef Debra Ponzek of Aux Délices, in Greenwich, Connecticut, is the ideal way to welcome the first chilly days of autumn. Split peas and potato are flavored with fresh vegetables and herbs, as well as smoky bacon and Black Forest ham, in a smooth, fragrant brew.

2 strips bacon, stacked and thinly sliced
    crosswise
1 stalk celery, thinly sliced
1 carrot, thinly sliced
1 small onion, thinly sliced
6 ounces split peas
2 teaspoons chopped fresh thyme

4 cups chicken or vegetable stock, or canned
    low-sodium chicken or vegetable broth
3 ounces Black Forest ham, cut into small dice
1 russet potato, peeled and cut into small dice
Kosher salt
Freshly ground black pepper

1. Heat a medium saucepan over medium heat for 2 to 3 minutes. Add the bacon and cook for 3 to 4 minutes. Add the celery, carrot, and onion, and sauté for 10 to 12 minutes, until the vegetables are softened. Add the split peas, thyme, and stock.

2. Increase the heat to high and bring the soup to a boil. Reduce the heat to medium and simmer for 30 to 35 minutes. Add the ham and potato, and simmer until the potato is soft, another 12 to 15 minutes. Season with salt and pepper to taste, and serve hot.

SUE TORRES

Chorizo, Potato, and Goat Cheese Quesadillas

Makes 4 to 6 quesadillas, each 1 serving

If you don't usually think of tortillas and potatoes together, these crisp, fragrant tortilla "sandwiches" from chef Sue Torres, of Manhattan's Sueño, will change your point of view. Spicy chorizo and hot poblanos make great companions for creamy potatoes, melting cheese, and fragrant herbs.

FOR THE PEPPERS:

2 red bell peppers, skin well dried with paper towels

2 poblano peppers, skin well dried with paper towels

Place the peppers over a high, open flame and turn until roasted and blackened on all sides. Cover with plastic wrap or put into a Ziploc bag and allow to cool for 15 to 20 minutes. Under a thin stream of cold running water, peel off the burned skin. Remove the stem. Split the pepper open and rinse out the seeds. Pat dry and cut into julienne. Reserve.

1 pound russet potatoes, unpeeled

Kosher salt

2 tablespoons olive oil

1 tablespoon unsalted butter

1 onion, thinly sliced

Freshly ground black pepper

1 pound chorizo, casing removed and cut into
     2$1/2$-inch pieces

1. Put the potatoes in a medium pot and cover with lightly salted water. Bring to a simmer over medium-high heat and cook for about 10 minutes. Reduce the heat to medium and cook until fork-tender, 30 to 35 minutes, depending on size. When cool enough to handle, peel and cut into small dice. Reserve.

2. In a medium skillet, heat 1 tablespoon of the olive oil and the butter over low heat until the butter has melted, and cook the onion until softened but not colored, about 20 minutes. Season with salt and pepper. Increase the heat to medium-low and continue cooking until the onion is golden. Remove to a bowl and reserve.

3. Return the skillet to medium-high heat and add the remaining 1 tablespoon olive oil. Cook the chorizo until browned, about 5 minutes. Cut into $1/4$-inch circles and quarter the circles. Reserve.

TO MAKE THE TORTILLAS:

$1/4$ cup shredded fresh cilantro

2 cups shredded Monterey Jack cheese

2 cups crumbled goat cheese, or substitute
     another 2 cups Monterey Jack

Kosher salt

Freshly ground black pepper

8 to 12 (12-inch) flour tortillas, or substitute
     corn tortillas

Vegetable oil

Crème fraîche or sour cream (optional)

Sliced radishes (optional)

1. Preheat the oven to 400°F.

2. In a large mixing bowl, combine the reserved red bell peppers, poblanos, potatoes, onion, and chorizo. Add the cilantro, Monterey Jack cheese, and goat cheese. Season with salt and pepper.

3. Lay 1 tortilla flat on a work surface and spread with about 1 cup of filling, making a 1/2-inch-thick layer. Top with another tortilla, to make a quesadilla. Repeat with the remaining tortillas and filling.

4. Arrange the filled quesadillas on ungreased baking sheets, 2 to a sheet, and bake until crisp, 12 minutes.

TO SERVE, cut each quesadilla into 4 wedges. Garnish with crème fraîche and sliced radishes, if desired.

Dutch Stamppot

Makes 6 servings

This satisfying winter dish (the name means "hodgepodge") is traditional in Holland, and comes to us from the kitchen of NL, Manhattan's Dutch restaurant. Hot, buttery mashed potatoes are combined with crisp bacon and fresh escarole, and topped with a layer of smoked sausage slices. Chef Pinxteren gilds the lily, and you can do the same, with a touch of truffle oil.

3 pounds russet potatoes, peeled
Kosher salt
1 pound kielbasa, preferably half beef
*   and half pork*
1 pound bacon
1/2 cup milk
4 tablespoons cold unsalted butter,
*   cut into 1/2-inch cubes*

1 teaspoon white truffle oil (optional;
*   see Sources)*
1 pound escarole, washed and leaves cut into
*   1-inch strips (or substitute watercress or*
*   arugula; see Note)*
Freshly ground black pepper
1 tablespoon chopped fresh chives

1. Cut the potatoes lengthwise into 4 pieces, and place them in a bowl of cold water, so they won't discolor. Put them in a large pot and cover with salted cold water. Cook over high heat until the water begins to boil, then reduce the heat to medium and simmer for 20 minutes, or until the potatoes are done, and they begin to fall apart when pressed with a fork.

2. Meanwhile, in a small saucepan, cover the sausage with hot water and cook over medium heat until warm. To prevent the sausage from cracking, do not let the water boil. Drain, and reserve the sausage in the pot.

3. In a large skillet over high heat, fry the bacon until crisp. Drain on paper towels and crumble into 1/2-inch pieces.

4. In a small saucepan over low heat, or in a microwavable cup, warm the milk. Set aside.

5. Drain the potatoes in a sieve, shaking them dry, and put them into a large bowl. Mash with a potato masher, or pass through a food mill or ricer, until they are light and fluffy. With a wooden spoon, stir in the cold cubes of butter, one at a time. When the butter is fully incorporated, add the milk and stir well. Add the truffle oil, if using.

6. Add the escarole and bacon to the potatoes and mix thoroughly with a wooden spoon. Add salt and pepper to taste, and spoon the mixture into a serving bowl.

7. Slice the sausage and arrange the slices decoratively over the potatoes. Sprinkle with the chives and serve.

NOTE: If desired, you can briefly sauté the escarole in 2 tablespoons olive oil with 1 clove garlic, finely chopped. If you are using watercress or arugula, do not sauté.

Bacon Lovers' Mashed Potatoes

PORK

Makes 10 servings

Chef Guarnaschelli, of the Manhattan restaurant Butter, tells us that the renowned chef Joachim Bernard Spilchal created this dish, a perfect accompaniment to any grilled or roasted meat or poultry. For true bacon and potato fans, it can be a meal in itself.

2 pounds Red Bliss potatoes, unpeeled, quartered

2 pounds Yukon Gold potatoes, peeled and quartered

Kosher salt

16 strips bacon, stacked and thinly sliced crosswise (see Note)

$1/4$ cup cold water

2 white onions, finely chopped

$1^1/2$ cups milk, plus more as needed

1 cup heavy cream

4 tablespoons unsalted butter

Freshly ground white pepper

2 tablespoons chopped fresh parsley (optional)

1. In a large pot, combine the Red Bliss and Yukon Gold potatoes. Fill the pot with water and bring to a boil over high heat; salt the water. Allow the potatoes to boil steadily until they are tender in the center when pierced with the tip of a knife.

2. Meanwhile, in a medium skillet, combine the sliced bacon and water (the water will draw some salt from the bacon). Cook over low heat until the water evaporates and the bacon is light brown and crisp. Add the onions, stirring with a wooden spoon to blend. Cook for 12 to 15 minutes, until the onions are tender. Drain any excess fat and set aside.

3. When the potatoes are tender, drain them in a colander, discarding the cooking water. Allow the potatoes to cool, and their excess liquid to drain off, for 5 minutes, but no longer. If the potatoes cool too much, the resulting dish can be gummy and elastic.

4. In a medium pot over medium heat, heat the milk, cream, and butter. In a large bowl, combine the potatoes with the milk mixture, mixing with a large whisk or a wooden spoon until the mixture is a chunky but homogeneous mass. Add the bacon and onions. Season to taste with salt and white pepper. Sprinkle with the parsley, if desired, and serve hot.

NOTE: If desired, set aside some of the cooked bacon and crumble it over the top of the potatoes just before serving.

Tartiflette de Cocotte (Potato Gratin with Cheese and Bacon)

Makes 4 to 6 servings

This "estimable early fall dinner" (*The New York Times*) comes from Chef William Snell of Brooklyn's Cocotte and LouLou restaurants. Departing from tradition, he adds garden-fresh zucchini and yellow squash to this popular French gratin. Serve the *tartiflette* with your favorite salad of delicate greens.

3 Yukon Gold potatoes, unpeeled,
    cut lengthwise into eighths
1 tablespoon chopped fresh tarragon
2 tablespoons chopped flat-leaf parsley
2 tablespoons canola oil
Kosher salt
Freshly ground black pepper
8 ounces very good quality bacon (preferably
    applewood smoked) strips, stacked and
    cut into 1/4-inch-wide pieces
1 cup small- to medium-diced seeded zucchini
1 cup small- to medium-diced seeded yellow
    squash

2 large Spanish onions, cut into small to
    medium dice
5 ounces shiitake mushrooms, stemmed and
    quartered (or substitute cremini or
    button mushrooms)
8 cloves garlic, very thinly sliced
1 (8 1/2 ounce) wheel of Reblochon cheese,
    halved lengthwise to form 2 disks
    (you may have to buy an 8 1/2-ounce
    portion of a larger wheel; if you can't
    find Reblochon, substitute Gruyère or
    Muenster)

1. Preheat the oven to 350°F.
2. In a mixing bowl, combine the potatoes, tarragon, 1 tablespoon of the parsley, and the canola oil, and season with a pinch of salt and pepper. Toss until most of the herbs

adhere to the potatoes. Put the potatoes into a shallow baking pan and roast for 30 to 35 minutes, until golden brown. Allow to cool slightly at room temperature.

3. Increase the oven temperature to 400°F.

4. In a large sauté pan over medium heat, cook the bacon until crisp but not well done, 6 to 10 minutes. Drain the bacon on paper towels, discarding all but 2 tablespoons of the bacon fat in the pan.

5. Add the zucchini, yellow squash, onions, and mushrooms to the reserved bacon fat. Cook over medium heat, stirring occasionally, for about 5 minutes. Add the garlic, season with salt and pepper, and cook, stirring constantly, for an additional 3 minutes (you may have to do this in batches; or use 2 pans, with slightly less fat in each pan). Remove the pan from the heat and stir in the reserved bacon.

6. Pour the vegetable mixture into a medium ovenproof casserole. Place the cheese disks on top, cut side down. Place in the oven for 12 to 15 minutes, until the cheese has completely melted and the rind is left on top of the vegetables. Let the *tartiflette* cool at room temperature for 3 minutes, sprinkle with the remaining 1 tablespoon parsley, and serve.

Roasted New Potatoes with Bacon, Chive Flowers, and Green Tomato Dressing

Makes 6 servings

Chef Rosen, of the City Bakery in Manhattan, created this light, herbaceous salad of roasted new potatoes with bacon. The nearby Union Square Greenmarket provided green tomatoes for the citric, fresh-tasting dressing, as well as beautiful chive flowers and greens. But even if you're not in the neighborhood, you can find most of these ingredients at your local market—and fresh chives can stand in for the flowers.

FOR THE GREEN TOMATO DRESSING:

3 small green tomatoes
1/4 cup plain rice vinegar (available at Asian markets and some supermarkets)
1 tablespoon seasoned rice vinegar (available at Asian markets and some supermarkets)

1 1/2 teaspoons Dijon mustard
3/8 cup canola oil
Kosher salt
Freshly ground black pepper

1. Bring a medium pot of water to a boil over high heat. Add the whole green tomatoes and cook for 10 minutes. Drain and allow to cool in a bowl of cold water. When they are cool enough to handle, peel, core, and quarter the tomatoes.

2. Put the tomatoes in a food processor, add the plain rice vinegar and the seasoned rice vinegar, and purée. With the machine running, add the mustard and drizzle in the canola oil. Season with salt and pepper. Can be refrigerated for up to 2 days.

1 1/2 pounds red new potatoes, unpeeled,
     halved or quartered, depending
     upon size
Canola oil
Kosher salt
Freshly ground black pepper
Green Tomato Dressing

5 to 8 strips bacon, stacked and cut into
     3/8-inch pieces, cooked and drained
12 purple chive flowers or 4 chives, cut into
     1-inch pieces
1 large handful of sturdy greens (such as
     arugula, escarole, bok choy, or spinach),
     washed

1. Preheat the oven to 350°F.

2. Toss the potatoes with canola oil to coat, and season with salt and pepper. Place the potatoes on a sheet tray in a single layer and roast for about 30 minutes, or until the cut sides are golden brown. Allow the potatoes to cool briefly.

3. In a large serving bowl, toss the potatoes with 1/2 cup of the Green Tomato Dressing. Add the bacon and chive flowers, reserving some flowers for garnish. Adjust the seasoning. In another bowl, toss the greens lightly with the remaining dressing, or to taste.

TO SERVE, divide the potato mixture among 6 plates and garnish with the greens and reserved chive flowers.

Chefs' Biographies

HUGH ACHESON, chef-owner of Five-and-Ten Restaurant, in Athens, Georgia, graduated high school in Ottawa, where his father is an economics professor, and studied political philosophy in college. He began his restaurant career as a dishwasher and cooked at various restaurants in Canada, all the while educating himself about food, wine, etiquette, food history, and food science. He was inspired by Chef Rob MacDonald of Ottawa's Cafe Henri Burger and followed him to Maplelawn Restaurant as sous-chef. Hugh moved to Athens, where he cooked at the Last Resort, while his wife, Mary, completed graduate studies at the University of Georgia. When she graduated, they moved to San Francisco, where Hugh worked with renowned chefs Mike Fennelly, at Mecca, and Gary Danko.

Returning to Athens, he opened Five-and-Ten and was named one of the Ten Best New Chefs of 2001 by *Food & Wine* magazine, which praised him for his success in "merging soul food with Old World cuisine."

DANIEL ANGERER, executive chef and owner of Fresh restaurant in Tribeca, was born in Austria and trained in Europe and the United States. He has worked with some of the world's most respected chefs and restaurateurs, including Joel Robouchon in Paris. He started his career in the Hotel Arlberg Hospiz, high in the mountains of Austria, and then moved on to Austria's Steirereck Restaurant. He moved to Germany, working under Heinz Winkler at the Relais & Chateaux. In America, Chef Angerer worked at Manhattan's San Domenico, Restaurant Jean Georges, and Bouley Bakery; and Palm Beach's Aquario.

In New York, Chef Angerer was associated with the French bistro Alouette, the bistro Barrio, and Steak Frites Restaurant.

MICHAEL ANTHONY, executive chef of Blue Hill Restaurant, in Manhattan, graduated at the top of his class from École Supérieure de Cuisine Française, in Paris. His love for cooking was fueled during his years in Japan, where he came to appreciate the clean and fresh Japanese aesthetic. In France, he trained at Chez Pauline, L'Auberge de Tal Moor, and Restaurant Jacques Cagna, where he met and worked with Dan Barber. In 1995, Restaurant Daniel brought Michael back to the United States, and two years later he became sous-chef, and then *chef de cuisine*. He joined Blue Hill in September 2001.

DAN BARBER, chef-owner of Manhattan's Blue Hill Restaurant and Dan Barber Catering, Inc., is a native New Yorker and a graduate of Tufts University. He began cooking for family and friends at Blue Hill Farm in the Berkshires, the home of his grandmother, where much of the produce for the restaurant and catering company is still grown. Dan apprenticed at Chez Panisse and Joe's, in California, and Michel Rostang and Apicus, in France. Dan opened Blue Hill in April 2000 and was named by *Food & Wine* magazine as one of America's Top New Chefs of 2002.

DIANA BARRIOS TREVIÑO has been a key player in her family's San Antonio restaurant, Los Barrios, since it opened in 1979. Diana is actively involved in the culinary media and has appeared on her local NBC station doing a live cooking segment, as well as on *FoodNation* with Bobby Flay and *Good Morning America* with Emeril Lagasse. She is the author of *Los Barrios Family Cookbook* (Villard, 2002). Diana is a member of Les Dames D'Escoffier and several local chambers of commerce. She is married to Roland Treviño and is the mother of Jordan, Evan, and Diego.

PHILIPPE BERTINEAU, executive chef of Payard Pâtisserie and Bistro, in Manhattan, was raised on his family's farm in the Poitou-Charentes region of France. His culinary study included several apprenticeships in the kitchens of Bordeaux, southwestern France, and the Basque region of France, including the prestigious Hôtel du Palais, in Biarritz. He traveled to London, where he spent a year at the Auberge de Provence, and then returned to France, where he spent another year at Restaurant Vanel, in Toulouse.

Moving to New York, Philippe became sous-chef for Park Bistro, and in 1993 joined Daniel Boulud for the opening of Daniel, where he was sous-chef until 1997. In August 1997, he became executive chef of Payard. In 1998, he received the White Truffle Award from the Italian Consulate in New York, and in 2001, *New York* magazine named him Best Unsung Chef.

JIM BOTSACOS, executive chef of Molyvos, in Manhattan, is a descendant of talented Greek-American and Italian-American chefs and is a graduate of Rhode Island's Johnson and Wales University. Starting his career at New York's "21" Club, he advanced from summer intern to saucier to sous-chef, and then became executive sous-chef. Also in New York, he was the first executive chef at the Park Avalon restaurant and was consulting chef at the Blue Water Grill. In 1997, with his move to Molyvos, he traveled to Greece to research the country's regional home cooking. *The New York Times* awarded Molyvos three stars in 1997, *Esquire* magazine's John Mariani named the restaurant among the "Best in America" that same year, and Molyvos made *New York* magazine's "Best of 1999" list. Chef Botsacos has appeared on network television on *The Early Show, Today,* and *Martha Stewart Living;* and on the TV Food Network on *Food Today* and *Cooking Live.* He was featured chef in *Bon Appétit* magazine's annual restaurant issue in September 2000.

ANTOINE BOUTERIN, executive chef and owner of Bouterin, on Manhattan's Upper East Side, was born on a historic farm in Saint-Rémy-de-Provence. Although he came from a family of farmers, he decided at the age of twelve to become a chef and soon afterward apprenticed at the two-star Riboto de Taven in Les-Baux-de-Provence. He honed his skills at the celebrated L'Escale, near Marseilles, among other fine restaurants, and moved to Paris, where, despite his youth, he became chef at the fashionable Quai d'Orsay. His next move was to Manhattan's Le Périgord, where he was executive chef from 1982 to 1995. He then opened the successful Bouterin, filling it with the art and food of his native Provence. Chef Bouterin is the author of *Cooking with Antoine at Le Périgord* (Putnam, 1986), *Antoine Bouterin's Desserts from Le Périgord* (Putnam, 1989), and *Cooking Provence* (Macmillan, 1994).

FRANK COE is the chef-owner of the Wild Goose, in Cutchogue, Long Island, which he runs with his wife, Barbara Sweeney. A native of Cork, Ireland, Frank has cooked in France, England, Australia, and several

Asian nations. In London, he owned two private dining clubs, Le Chasse and the Funny Farm. In Manhattan, he worked at Daniel, Le Bernardin, and Can, and he owned and operated the award-winning Druids in Manhattan's Hell's Kitchen neighborhood.

Frank's mother, Elizabeth Mellerick, was a pastry chef in France and Switzerland, and his love of cooking began in her kitchen when he was only six years old. At seventeen, he traveled to Lyons, France, to study cooking, and almost ten years later, he went to Singapore, where he cooked for six months. His cuisine is based on the finest of seasonal foods, which have inspired him since he picked herbs and vegetables in his family's garden as a child. His inspiration comes from the market and from the various cultures he has explored as a chef.

RON CRISMON, chef-owner of the Tribeca restaurant Bubby's Pie Company, is a native New Yorker. He trained in a traditional apprenticeship program, held restaurant jobs in Atlanta, and was sous-chef for the Hyatt Corporation. Ron had been working as a catering chef in Manhattan when he decided to open Bubby's in 1990, at age twenty-eight.

The restaurant's combination of homey warmth and downtown funkiness has, from the start, attracted high-profile diners from the worlds of entertainment and politics. It is acclaimed for its home-cooked American food, especially its pies, breakfast, brunch, meat loaf, and barbecue. Ron says, "I've been cooking meat and potatoes since I started to crawl." Ron is the creator of Loco Soda, a fruit juice–based soft drink with a surprise kick: fresh chili peppers. The electrifying drink is available in lime, mango, blackberry, and raspberry flavors.

CRAIG CUPANI, a 1988 graduate of the Culinary Institute of America, has most recently been executive chef at Manhattan's Patroon restaurant. Also in Manhattan, he served as *chef de cuisine* at the Brasserie, sous-chef at Tabla, executive chef/general manager at Butterfield 81, executive sous-chef (under Chef Michael Lomonoco) at the "21" Club, and roundsman (under Chef John Doherty) at the Waldorf-Astoria. His food is "creative American," based on the highest-quality ingredients available, prepared with skill and imagination.

ANDREW DICATALDO, executive chef of Manhattan's celebrated Patria, is a graduate of Johnson & Wales University. He cooked at the Hyatt Regency Hotel in Miami and at South Beach's ultrahip Scratch Restaurant, where he was introduced to local Florida produce and Latino ingredients. In 1990, Andrew became executive sous-chef at Yuca, Miami's famous Nuevo Cubano restaurant, and from there moved to Manhattan's Patria, first as *chef de cuisine* and then, in 1999, as executive chef. He is tenacious about finding the finest, freshest ingredients, and has been praised for his deft handling of spices and flavors. William Grimes, the *New York Times* restaurant critic, found him deserving of "a double round of applause" as well as a three-star rating, and Patria has been voted best pan-Latino restaurant for three consecutive years by *Time Out New York* magazine.

KEITH DRESSER is currently a test cook and member of the editorial staff at *Cook's Illustrated* magazine, and has been cooking on New England's coast for his entire career. He has been sous-chef at Boston's Red Clay and executive chef of the Regatta of Falmouth, in Massachusetts. He has cooked at Hamersley's Bistro in Boston's South End and at Eat, in Somerville. Keith studied at the New England Culinary Institute in Montpelier, Vermont, and at Harvard University.

BOBBY FLAY, chef and partner of Manhattan's popular Mesa Grill and Bolo, began working at the Joe Allen Restaurant at age seventeen, where he so impressed the management that Joe Allen paid his tuition to the prestigious French Culinary Institute. After working with restaurateur Jonathan Waxman, Bobby moved to Manhattan's Miracle Grill and raised it to near-cult status with his colorful southwestern creations. Bobby's own Mesa Grill opened in 1991, followed by Bolo, dedicated to exploring Spanish cuisine, in 1993.

In 1993, Bobby was voted the James Beard Foundation's Rising Star Chef of the Year, and the French Culinary Institute honored him with its first Outstanding Graduate Award. He is the author of *Bobby Flay's Bold American Food* (Warner Books, 1994), *Bobby Flay's From My Kitchen to Your Table* (Crown, 1998), *Bobby Flay's Boy Meets Grill* (Hyperion, 1999), and *Bobby Flay Cooks American* (Hyperion, 2001). He is well known to television viewers for his popular shows *Grillin' and Chillin'*, *The Main Ingredient*, *Hot Off the Grill*, *Boy Meets Grill*, and *FoodNation*.

LAURA FRANKEL, owner and executive chef of Shallots gourmet kosher restaurants in Manhattan and Chicago, is a graduate of Northwestern University, the Cooking Hospitality Institute of Chicago, and the French Pastry School at City Colleges of Chicago. Her restaurants have been enthusiastically reviewed in the Chicago press.

After extensive professional kitchen experience, Chef Frankel took a respite to have a family (she is the mother of three) and then returned and opened Shallots in Chicago. One year later, she opened Shallots NY. She is now working on a cookbook and contemplating the production of a packaged-food product.

MARK FRANZ, executive chef and co-owner of Farallon in San Francisco, is a graduate of the California Culinary Academy and a third-generation restaurateur. He has cooked at Jeremiah Tower's Stars Restaurant and Balboa Café, and Ernie's, in San Francisco, and the Santa Fe Bar and Grill, in Berkeley. Under Mark's stewardship, Farallon has been nominated by the James Beard Foundation as one of the best restaurants in the United States, has been chosen one of the best newcomers by *Esquire, Bon Appétit,* and *Food & Wine* magazines, and was the highest-rated newcomer in the 1999 *Zagat Survey.*

MARK GAIER and CLARK FRASIER, chef-owners of Arrows Restaurant in Ogunquit, Maine, have created a classic country restaurant that has garnered enthusiastic reviews in *USA Today, Wine Spectator, Town & Country, Bon Appétit,* and *Boston Magazine,* among others, and was named one of America's Fifty Best Restaurants of 2001 by *Gourmet* magazine.

Clark grew up in Carmel, California—fresh-produce heaven, where vegetables and fruit are available all year round. When he went to China to study Chinese, he developed expertise in the cuisine of China and learned "why food tastes so good when it is in season." He moved to San Francisco to set up an import-export business but instead went to work at Jeremiah Tower's Stars Restaurant, where he became *chef tournant.* There he met Mark Gaier, who was to become his partner in Arrows in 1988.

Mark, who grew up near Dayton, Ohio, was inspired by his mother, a wonderful cook. He worked in publishing in Blue Hill, Maine, and then studied culinary arts under Jean Wallach in Boston. Later, working at the Whistling Oyster, under Mark Allen, he developed many of his skills as a chef. In the mid-eighties, he joined the staff at Stars Restaurant, as *chef tournant.*

SANDRO GAMBA, *chef de cuisine* for the Park Hyatt Hotel in Chicago and its restaurant, NoMI, was previously executive chef at Lespinasse, in Washington, D.C., where he was selected as one of the World's Best Chefs by the American Academy of Hospitality Sciences. Named by *Food & Wine* magazine as one of America's Top New Chefs of 2001, he has worked extensively in both France and the United States and has trained under Alain Ducasse, at Le Louis XV; Joel Robouchon, at Le Jamin; and Roger Verge, at Le Moulin de Mougins. His grandmother Jeannette, the chef-owner of Les Cinq Ponts, in Neufchâteau, France, was a strong influence on his cuisine, teaching him that simplicity and authenticity should be his goals in cooking.

JEAN-LOUIS GERIN, chef-owner of Restaurant Jean-Louis, in Greenwich, Connecticut, has been widely praised for his fresher, lighter, more intensely flavored versions of classic cuisine, "La Nouvelle Classique." He was born in Annecy in the French Alps, and both his father and his grandfather were talented amateur chefs.

When his family moved to Talloires, thirteen-year-old Jean-Louis took a summer job at the Michelin three-star Auberge du Père Bis. He later received formal restaurant training and a degree in business from l'École Hôteliere de Thonon les Bains, and then returned to Auberge du Père Bise to continue his apprenticeship.

Jean-Louis later worked at the three-star Oustau de Beaumanière and, along with his friend Chef Guy Savoy, at La Barriere de Clichy, in Paris. The two opened Guy Savoy in Paris, where Jean-Louis became Savoy's assistant in charge of purchasing and staff. In 1984, Jean-Louis joined Savoy's chic French restaurant in Greenwich, and by 1985 had agreed to purchase the restaurant, renaming it Restaurant Jean-Louis. In 1986, Jean-Louis married Linda Chardain, daughter of restaurateur Rene Chardain.

LAURENT GRAS, executive chef at San Francisco's renowned Fifth Floor, at the Hotel Palomar, is a native of France's Côte d'Azur, where he grew up with fruit orchards, the freshest fish from the Mediterranean, and a family olive grove where oil was pressed every December.

Beginning at age eighteen, he spent seven years in French Michelin-starred kitchens and then became *chef de cuisine* at Restaurant Guy Savoy in Paris for two years. Next, he spent five years as *chef de cuisine* for Alain Ducasse at Restaurant Alain Ducasse and Hôtel de Paris, where he achieved three Michelin stars. In 1997, Gras headed for New York and the executive chef position at the Waldorf-Astoria's Peacock Alley, where he quickly earned three stars from *New York Times* critic Ruth Reichl.

In November 2001, Chef Gras moved to California and immediately researched the area's best producers, explored its restaurants, and immersed himself in the local culture while evolving his menu. At Fifth Floor, Gras has achieved a culinary maturity based on experience, world travels, and talent. He credits the influence of his mentors—Jacques Maximin, Alain Ducasse, and Alain Senderen. He also adheres to his three personal principles: "Flavor, aesthetic, and perfection, in that order."

ALEXANDRA GUARNASCHELLI, chef at Butter, in Manhattan, has been an instructor in both professional and recreational cooking at the Institute of Culinary Education. She began her career in 1992 at Manhattan's An American Place, cooking with Larry Forgione and Richard D'Orazi. She moved to France, where she trained at La Varenne and L'Essential. In Paris, she became *chef de partie* at Guy Savoy, and later, sous-chef at La Butte Chaillot. Alexandra assisted Patricia Wells with her book *Patricia Wells at Home in Provence* and with Patricia's publication *L'Atelier of Joël Robouchon*.

Returning to the United States in 1997, Alexandra became *chef de partie,* and later, sous-chef, at Daniel Boulud's Daniel. She then worked as sous-chef at Joachim Bernard Spilchal's Patina, and finally returned to New York, with Chef Spilchal, to open Nick & Stef's Steakhouse, first as sous-chef and then as executive chef, where she remained until 2002.

GLENN HARRIS, executive chef and partner at Jane, in Manhattan, began his lifelong interest in cooking as a child in his mother's Coney Island kitchen. By the age of twelve, he was working part-time in a local Chinese restaurant, and by the time he was seventeen, he was a partner in a small but successful local eatery. After graduation from the French Culinary Institute, Glenn worked at several popular New York restaurants, and in 1995 was hired by Jonathan Waxman (then of Ark restaurants) to take over the Museum Cafe. He later became the opening chef at Ark's acclaimed Bryant Park Grill. In April 2001, he opened Jane Restaurant with Jeffrey Lefcourt.

GERRY HAYDEN, executive chef and partner of Manhattan's Amuse restaurant, is a graduate of the Culinary Institute of America. He became sous-chef and pastry chef when Charlie Palmer opened Aureole in 1988. Gerry moved to Tribeca Grill in 1990 as Don Pintabona's sous-chef, and then to San Francisco as sous-chef under Chef George Morrone. He returned to New York to head up Drew Nieporent's East Hampton Point and was then hired as executive chef of Marguery Grill (which *Esquire* magazine named Best New Restaurant, under Gerry's leadership). In 1999, he returned to Aureole as *chef de cuisine,* and in 2003, opened Amuse.

THOMAS JOHN, executive chef of Mantra, in Boston, grew up in southern India with a two-acre garden behind his house, and learned early on from his parents the connection between freshness and taste. Herbs, seeds, vegetables, and fruits were plucked just minutes before use, whether for traditional holiday feasts or just for lunch on Monday. In his cooking, Chef John uses a subtle hand to introduce the cornucopia of Indian spices to the freshest foods available. Using French technique, he aims for a sophisticated palate that blends accessibility with exoticism. America's agricultural bounty provides him with an almost limitless pantry of ingredients from which to create, in his words, "like a mad Indian scientist."

A graduate of Punjab University and the Oberoi School of Hotel Management, Chef John cooked at the Oberoi Hotel in Delhi, where his recipes became the basis for the hotel's *Food of India* cookbook. Shortly thereafter, he was named executive chef of Le Meridien, in Pune, where he oversaw the property's four international restaurants, including Spice Island, a concept he developed to showcase India's lesser-known flavors.

Esquire magazine named Mantra one of the Top New Restaurants of 2001, and *Food & Wine* magazine named Chef Thomas John one of America's Top New Chefs of 2001. His cuisine has been praised by *The Wall*

Street Journal, the *Economist*, *InStyle*, *Details*, *Bon Appétit*, *Travel & Leisure*, *Town & Country*, *Architecture*, and the *Robb Report*.

MATTHEW KENNEY has been executive chef and owner of Commissary NY in Manhattan; Commissary, in Portland, Maine; Commune Atlanta; and Nickerson Tavern, in Searsport, Maine. He is a graduate of the French Culinary Institute and in 1995 was granted its Outstanding Graduate Award, as well as being named PBS Rising Star Chef. In 1994 and 1995, he was nominated for the James Beard Foundation's Rising Star Chef Award, and he was recognized by *Food & Wine* magazine in 1994 as one of the Ten Best New Chefs in America. He is the author of *Matthew Kenney's Mediterranean Cooking* (Chronicle Books, 1997) and *Matthew Kenney's Big City Cooking* (Chronicle Books, 2003).

LEVANA KIRSCHENBAUM, chef and founder of Manhattan's Levana Restaurant, Tableclassics catering service, and Levana's Place gourmet kosher cooking school, was born and raised in Morocco and learned to cook and appreciate exotic cuisine at her mother's side. She earned a degree in psychology from the Sorbonne, and traveled to Spain and Israel, where she added to her extensive repertoire of multicultural dishes.

Levana has conducted master cooking classes at the Natural Gourmet Institute for Food and Health, Macy's New York, the Ninety-second Street Y, and the Sephardic Center Cooking Institute. She has appeared on the PBS television series *The United Tastes of America* and WOR radio's *Food Talk*, with Arthur Schwartz. She is the author of *Levana's Table: Kosher Cooking for Everyone* (Stewart, Tabori & Chang, 2002).

ANITA LO, chef and owner (with partner Jennifer Scism) of Annisa Restaurant, in Manhattan's West Village, was born in Michigan and studied French at Columbia University. In the summer of her junior year, Anita traveled to France to study cooking, and immediately after graduation, she went to work at Bouley Restaurant. Returning to France, she earned her degree in cooking at the Ritz-Escoffier School, graduating with honors. Anita then served internships at several Paris restaurants, under such noted chefs as Michel Rostang and Guy Savoy. She moved to Manhattan's Chanterelle, where she worked through all the stations, and next became the chef of Can, a French-Vietnamese restaurant in SoHo. There she met Jennifer Scism, who was the sous-chef.

Anita spent two and a half years as chef at Maxim's and then moved to Mirezi Restaurant, where she won rave reviews, followed by television appearances on NBC, CNN, and Food Network. *Avenue Asia* magazine named her one of the 500 Most Influential Asian-Americans. After two years, she left Mirezi and traveled with Jennifer through Southeast Asia and Mediterranean Europe, planning their future restaurant, Annisa.

MITCHEL LONDON, owner of Mitchel London Foods, a prepared foods, catering, and pastry shop with three branches in Manhattan, is a graduate of and former teacher at the Rhode Island School of Design's Culinary Arts School. He served for seven years as chef to Mayor Ed Koch and is the author of *Mitchel London's Gracie Mansion Cookbook* (Contemporary Books, 1989). In addition to retail and catering, Mitchel London Foods is a purveyor of pastries to fine-food emporiums such as Dean & DeLuca and Balducci's. Mitchel also acts as a consultant to the prepared foods, pastry, and café departments at Fairway Market in Manhattan.

PHILIP MCGRATH is the chef-owner of the Iron Horse Grill in Pleasantville, New York, with his wife, Catherine Coreale, and they are also principals in Creative Culinary Consultants. Chef McGrath earned a B.S. degree from St. Francis College in Brooklyn Heights, and graduated first in his class from the Culinary Institute of America.

He has been executive chef at the Castle at Tarrytown and its award-winning Equus Restaurant. His culinary background includes positions at the Doubles Club, Prunelle, the Sign of the Dove, Glorious Foods, the Ritz Cafe, the Carlyle Hotel, and Jean-Jacques Rachou's Le Levandou and La Côte Basque, all in Manhattan. During visits to France, he worked at Restaurant Troisgros, in Roanne; L'Esperance, in St. Pere Sous Vezelay, and Restaurant Michel Rostang, in Paris.

Chef McGrath has been a lecturer at NYU's Hotel and Restaurant Management Certificate Program and has a cable television show, *Cooking with the Iron Horse*.

HENRY ARCHER MEER made an early career choice, and his classical training at the Culinary Institute of America led him to the legendary La Côte Basque, where he worked for over eight years. He then moved to Lutèce and cooked alongside Chef André Soltner for ten years, the last four as sous-chef. He opened SoHo's Cub Room in 1994 and in 1998 opened City Hall Restaurant—the quintessential New York eatery—in a landmark Tribeca building. Here he has re-created classic New York cuisine and added a clever, contemporary twist.

Chef Meer works with farmers in the tristate area to strengthen the important farm/restaurant relationship, and participates in Chefs Collaborative and the Council on the Environment of New York City, which operates the local greenmarkets.

CARLA PELLEGRINO is executive chef and co-owner of Baldoria, in the heart of Manhattan's theater district. Baldoria (which means "festivity" in Italian) is co-owned by her husband, Frank Pellegrino, Jr., whose family has operated Rao's, in east Harlem, since 1896. Carla was born in Brazil and moved to Liguria, in northern Italy, at the age of seventeen. She learned to cook from her mother and owned a boutique catering company in Italy before moving to New York. Her dream was to have her own restaurant, and with that goal, she graduated from New York's French Culinary Institute. Her creations for Baldoria have been highly praised in the press.

MAARTEN PINXTEREN was born in Amsterdam, Holland, and began his culinary career at age seventeen, in 1990, at Restaurant Vertigo. After completing an apprenticeship at the one-hundred-year-old Dikker en Thijs Hotel, he went on to serve as sous-chef in several popular Amsterdam restaurants, as well as in Cafe Bahia, in Portugal. Maarten became head chef of Cafe Toussaint in Amsterdam in 2000 and moved across the Atlantic in 2001 to be head chef of Restaurant NL, in Manhattan. He is currently working in the Netherlands.

DEBRA PONZEK, chef and owner of Aux Délices gourmet prepared foods shops in Greenwich, Connecticut, has received accolades for her innovative and subtle Provençal-inspired cuisine. Her early interest in cooking was nurtured by her mother and grandmother, but it wasn't until Debra was an engineering student at Boston University that she decided to pursue a career as a chef. She enrolled in the Culinary Institute of America and, after graduating in 1984, worked in top New Jersey restaurants. She was then hired by Drew Nieporent as sous-chef at Montrachet, in Manhattan, and soon was promoted to chef, a position she held for seven years. Under her stewardship, Montrachet earned three consecutive three-star reviews from *The New York Times*.

Debra was named a *Food & Wine* magazine Best New Chef of 1990 and a James Beard Foundation Rising Star Chef of the Year in 1991. She was the first American to receive the Moreau Award for culinary excellence from the Frederick Wildman and Sons Company. Debra is the author of *The Summer House Cookbook* (Clarkson Potter, 2003) and *French Food, American Accent: Debra Ponzek's Spirited Cuisine* (Clarkson Potter, 1996).

WALTER POTENZA, chef and owner of Rhode Island's Sunflower Café, in Cranston, and La Locanda del Coccio, A Pranzo, Aquaviva, and Zucchero, all in Providence, was born in Abruzzo, Italy. He is a respected master of Italian-Jewish cuisine, as well as the art of terra-cotta cookery, a method invented by the Etruscans three hundred years before the Roman Empire.

Chef Potenza is the director of Etruria International Cooking School in Gubbio, Italy, and Providence, Rhode Island; the president of Italcuochi America; the president of Accadèmia Italiana della Cucina, New England chapter; the president of the Rhode Island Culinary Educational Center; a food master of the Italian Culinary Institute; and a member of the "Italia a Tavola" Committee, an organization dedicated to the preservation and diffusion of the Italian culture in the United States. He has appeared in national and international publications and on television and radio, and is the host of the cable television show *Stir It Up*.

NORA POUILLON is chef and owner of Nora—the first certified organic restaurant in the country—and Asia Nora, both in Washington, D.C. Born in Vienna, she moved to the United States in 1965 and operated a catering business and a cooking school before opening her first restaurant.

Chef Pouillon has consulted and developed products for Green Circle Organics, Fresh Fields

Wholefoods Market, and Walnut Acres. She is a founding member of Chefs Collaborative, a leading spokesperson for the National Resources Defense Council (NRDC)/SeaWeb "Give North Atlantic Swordfish a Break" campaign; a member of the Organic Trade Association; a member of the advisory board of Foodfit.com; and a participant in the Harvard School of Public Health Nutrition Roundtable discussions.

Her book, *Cooking with Nora* (Random House, 1996), was a finalist for the Julia Child Cookbook Award for a first book. Among her many honors, Nora was given the Chef of the Year Award of Excellence by the International Association of Culinary Professionals (IACP) and was chosen as one of the dozen "power chefs" in Washington, D.C., by *The Washington Post*.

CYRIL RENAUD was born in a small town on the Brittany coast, where family and food were the center of life, and by the age of seven, he knew he wanted to become a chef. He began his culinary training in fine restaurants throughout Europe, and coming to the United States, he worked at Cellar in the Sky, on top of the World Trade Center, which he left in 1993. He moved on to the original Bouley, as *chef de cuisine*, and then became the youngest chef at La Caravelle, at age twenty-seven. In 1999, he was nominated for the James Beard Foundation's Rising Star Chef of the Year Award.

After leaving La Caravelle, he concentrated on painting—working in acrylic and watercolor, and using windowpanes from turn-of-the-century brownstones in his artistic creations. His artwork now adorns the walls of Fleur de Sel, in Manhattan. The interior structure of the restaurant, as well as the decor, was refurbished by his father, and the salt mills on each table were handpicked and brought from France by his mother.

ILENE ROSEN is a graduate of the French Culinary Institute. In her first professional job in the food industry, as savory chef of the City Bakery in Manhattan, she has established herself as a fearless new talent. Ilene is possessed by the bounty of the Union Square Greenmarket, and she routinely stalks New York's Chinatown with fervor and joy, in search of new foods to work with. She takes exotic as well as familiar ingredients and cooks clear, distinct, assured foods that have won her a loyal and growing following in downtown Manhattan.

FELINO SAMSON, partner and executive chef of Boston's Bomboa, was born in the Philippines and raised in Michigan. He is a graduate of Michigan State University and the Fashion Institute of Technology, and spent nine years working in the fashion industry. Turning his talents to the culinary world, he joined the staff of Manhattan's Sign of the Dove and subsequently became *chef de cuisine* at Boston's La Bettola and executive chef of Galleria Italiana.

In 1999, Samson entered Shreve, Crump, & Lowe's Edible Art Festival, and his prosciutto-covered Botero-inspired sculpture was judged as best overall entry. Several of his edible art pieces have been featured on television programs. That same year, Felino joined Bomboa, whose food has been featured in *Art Culinaire*, *Food & Wine*, *Bon Appétit*, and *People* magazines and has won the *Wine Spectator* Award of Excellence.

ARTHUR SCHWARTZ is a cookbook author and cooking teacher, and the host of *Food Talk*, a daily program heard on WOR radio in the New York City metropolitan area. His website is appropriately called www.thefoodmaven.com.

All four of his cookbooks have been nominated for national awards: *Cooking in a Small Kitchen* (Little Brown, 1978), *What to Cook When You Think There's Nothing in the House to Eat* (HarperCollins, 1992 and 2000), *Soup Suppers* (HarperCollins, 1994), and *Naples at Table: Cooking in Campania* (HarperCollins, 1998). He is working on a history of food in New York City to be published by Stewart, Tabori and Chang in 2004.

Schwartz has written for numerous magazines, including *The New York Times Magazine*, *Saveur*, *Food & Wine*, *Gourmet*, *Cuisine*, *Vintage*, *Vogue*, *Lui*, *Playbill*, *Great Recipes*, and *Travel-Holiday*. He has appeared on the Food Network, the Learning Channel, Discovery Channel, the Lifetime Network, New York's *MetroGuide*, *Good Day New York*, *Live with Regis*, and many public television cooking programs. He has lectured and conducted seminars at New York University, Columbia University, New York City Technical College, the French Culinary Institute, and the Culinary Institute of America (CIA). He teaches and lectures at the major cooking schools in the metro New York area.

WILLIAM SNELL is executive chef and owner, with his wife, Christine, of Cocotte, in Brooklyn's Park Slope, and of Loulou, in Fort Greene—named after their young daughter. As a child in New Jersey, William learned to hunt and fish with his father, and he decided at an early age that he wanted to be a chef. He began his formal training in New Brunswick's Frog and the Peach Restaurant, and moved to the Tribeca Grill to work with Don Pintabona. He then became *chef de cuisine* at City Wine & Cigar Co., where he met Christine, a native of Brittany and a graduate of l'École Parisienne d'Hôtesses et de Tourisme. William also worked at Oran Nor, on Nantucket, and consulted in New York before opening his own restaurants.

DEBORAH STANTON is chef and owner of Deborah, in Greenwich Village, which has been praised by the New York *Daily News* as "over the top American, both in style and generosity." Deborah had previously been chef at Galaxy, in Manhattan, CHOW, in Miami's South Beach, and Woo Lae Oak, in SoHo, and has received rave reviews from *The New York Times, Food & Wine, New York* magazine, *Time Out New York, Paper* magazine, *Metrosource,* and *Art Culinaire.* Her career was temporarily halted when she was struck by an automobile, rendering her completely disabled. But after several surgeries and more than a year of treatment, she has returned to work with strength and determination.

JOHN SUNDSTROM, executive chef at Seattle's Earth and Ocean, was named a *Food & Wine* Best New Chef of 2001. Originally from Salt Lake City, John learned cooking in a Japanese restaurant and sushi bar, before graduating with honors from the New England Culinary Institute in Montpelier, Vermont. He then worked in prominent hotels, including the Ritz-Carlton Laguna Niguel, Club XIX at the Lodge at Pebble Beach, and the Stein Ericksen Lodge.

In Seattle, John began cooking at Raison d'Être Cafe, where he established contacts with local farmers. After stints at Café Sport and Campagne, John became sous-chef and then executive chef at the Dahlia Lounge.

In March 1999, John toured Japan, researching Japanese food and culture, and in October and November of that year, in New York and San Francisco, he worked with renowned chefs Daniel Boulud, Jean-George Vongerichten, Gary Danko, and Traci Des Jardins. He then ran the kitchen at Carmelita, in Seattle, before taking the top spot at Earth and Ocean.

ALLEN SUSSER established Chef Allen's Restaurant in Miami Beach in 1986. After earning degrees from New York City Technical College and Le Cordon Bleu, he worked at the Bristol Hotel in Paris and went on to other kitchens in Florida and New York, most notably that of Le Cirque. His highly praised cuisine encompasses the foods, cultures, and techniques of the Mediterranean, the Americas, Asia, and India. Among his many honors: Honorary Doctor of Culinary Arts, Johnson and Wales University; National Advisory Board, James Beard Foundation; *Gourmet* magazine's Top Table in South Florida, 2000; Best Chef, Southeastern Region, James Beard Foundation, 1994; number one restaurant for food and most popular in Miami, 1999 *Zagat Survey*; National Board of Directors, American Institute of Wine and Food. He is the author of *New World Cuisine and Cookery* (Doubleday, 1995) and *The Great Citrus Book* (Ten Speed Press, 1997).

SUE TORRES is the chef of Sueño, in Chelsea. She has been the executive chef of Hell's Kitchen, in the Manhattan neighborhood of the same name, where she introduced her own "progressive Mexican" cuisine. A graduate of the Culinary Institute of America, where she was a co-founder of its Saucier Club, she served her externship at the "21" Club. She worked in the kitchens of La Grenouille, Lola, and Steve Hanson's Isabella's, where she was a sous-chef at the age of twenty-one. She then moved to Arizona 206, where she became aware of the many ingredients and possibilities of Mexican food, and later became executive chef of the Rocking Horse Cafe Mexicana. Sue traveled to Mexico to study classic Mexican fare with Diana Kennedy.

Working Woman magazine has chosen Sue as one of the "20 under 30" successful American women. She is active in Share Our Strength and the James Beard Taste Makers, and she works with inner-city children in the Days of Taste and Dinner Party programs.

PATRICIA YEO has been co-executive chef of the restaurants AZ and Pazo, in Manhattan. She is a native of Eugene, Oregon, and a graduate of Princeton University, where she earned her doctorate in biochemistry, and the New York Restaurant School. In 1989, during a break in her postdoctoral studies, she took a cooking class and was inspired to turn in her lab coat for chef whites.

At culinary school, Patricia met Bobby Flay, who was then at Miracle Grill and hired her upon her graduation. When Bobby opened Mesa Grill in 1991, Patricia became sous-chef. She then moved to the West Coast to work at Barbara Tropp's China Moon. Patricia returned to Manhattan in 1993, as sous-chef of Flay's restaurant Bolo, where she worked for two years. She later opened San Francisco's Hawthorne Lane, under Chef Anne Gingrass, and after three years, she set off to explore Asia.

In 2000, Patricia opened AZ, to rave reviews from *New York* magazine, the *New York Observer*, *The New York Times*, the *New York Daily News*, and the *New York Post*. She opened the popular Pazo in 2002, and is the author of *Cooking from A to Z* (St. Martin's Press, 2002).

Index

A B O U T   T H E   A U T H O R

JOAN SCHWARTZ is an avid reader, writer, and cook, and the author and
co-author of twelve acclaimed cookbooks, including *Macaroni and Cheese:
52 Recipes, from Simple to Sublime; Matthew Kenney's Big City Cooking;*
Bobby Flay's *Bold American Food, Boy Meets Grill,* and *From My Kitchen to
Your Table;* and Joel Patraker's *Greenmarket Cookbook.* She is a graduate of
Rutgers University and received an M.A. from the University of Chicago. She is
listed in *Who's Who in America.* Joan lives in Westchester County, New York.